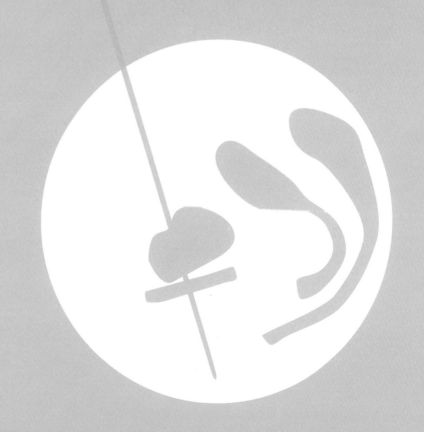

RICE TABLE

for Kiki
so you are never homesick

SU SCOTT

RICE TABLE

Korean recipes + stories
to feed the soul

Hardie Grant

QUADRILLE

SU SCOTT

a family that eats together stays together

It is true when they say the moment a child is born, the mother is also born. Motherhood and being an immigrant woman of certain age is an interesting mix, I concluded.

I was born and raised in Seoul, Korea and came to London alone in 2000. As a young girl a few months shy of turning twenty, I had left a home that I never really felt I belonged to and was eager to dive deep into my newfound freedom and immerse myself fully in London life. I didn't want to be recognized as a foreigner; I desperately wanted to be accepted by the city I had fallen madly in love with. Twenty-two years on, I call London my home, I am married to an English guy I met in a pub eighteen years ago, and now raise a child of dual heritage who looks and acts exactly half like me and half like her father.

But the birth of my daughter in 2015 left me feeling deeply lonely and homesick. Having spent all my adult life in the UK, motherhood made me feel confused about my identity as an immigrant and a mother. I was a Korean living in London, but when I went back home I was also a foreigner visiting Korea. Twenty-two years of being so far away, with very few visits in between and even fewer interactions with anyone who even remotely reminded me of home, had been enough to make me naturally drift away and lose a lot of what made me Korean. Gosh, was I that desperate to integrate? Even at the cost of losing my own sense of identity?

After so many years of living in London, to be faced with the truth – that I neither felt Korean nor British – was a difficult moment for me. Beyond that, the stark realization that I, as an immigrant mother, bore the sole duty to pass on the culture of my Korean heritage to my daughter hit me hard and weighed heavily on my heart, raising some fundamental questions.

I wanted to tell her the stories of where I come from and why I am here. I wanted us to cook the kind of food my mother fed me as a child and taste my childhood together. I wanted to speak the language my mother spoke and whisper our secrets to each other in the most intimate and loving ways I remember sharing with my own mother as a child.

But truth be told, everything felt like a real effort – all very alien and almost unnatural.

I really wanted my daughter to feel connected to my home, my family and where I come from. But so much of my own heritage and Koreanness had been lost in the name of integration, including the comfort of my own mother tongue.

It felt so strange to speak to my daughter in Korean, it often made me feel ashamed.

How was I supposed to tell my child what the other half of her blood is made of if I was unsure of who I am as a mother?

I missed the connection and familiarity of the land I was born and raised in; the soil I walked on, the culture and the people. I was so far removed from it all that I felt a deep void. So, to satisfy that longing, I started to cook the dishes I remembered from my childhood. I read and researched, and felt comforted by the tiny nuances I picked up between the lines. Then I got hungry for more. I dug deeper into the memories, craving that last taste of something I had eaten, desperate for some kind of connection, the warm embrace of something familiar. The perpetual cycle of hunger haunted me as I yearned for a sense of belonging.

It was becoming a mother that had made me realize the importance of continuing to cook dishes that connect me deeply to my roots, allowing me to restore my sense of a Korean heritage. After all, it is my daughter's birthright, and it is my duty to share the recipes from my family and traditions, ensuring she is entirely familiar with them and rooted in both sides of the cultures she has inherited.

My father's phrase, 'A family that eats together stays together', held great meaning for me throughout this personal journey, in both physical and metaphorical terms. Cooking and sharing the food of my origins – the dishes of my childhood homes and memories – truly helped me to reconnect to my long-forgotten Korean home.

Food allows us to remember and celebrate our inherent roots and feel a sense of belonging, however far we may be from home. And this is my story of reconnecting to my Korean roots. It's also a love letter to my daughter spoken through the dishes of my childhood that I cook in my tiny London kitchen where love is spoken tenderly through the memories of taste.

Our family kitchen of two halves and our love for food has reshaped and redefined what Korean food means to us. Food is the language of love my family chose, both here and back home in Korea. It is the language I choose to love my daughter the Korean way, because it is the only language that I speak fluently.

I really hope you will find your own stories in here somewhere and feel comforted in knowing that we all belong here.

Su x

Making Friends with Korean Ingredients

I believe cooking is about accessibility, and I try to keep things simple at home. It is helpful that the popularity of Korean food has steadily grown more mainstream over recent years and sourcing Korean ingredients has become a lot easier for most of us. I hope these few notes will fill in any gaps in your knowledge about the ingredients and their uses.

There aren't many unusual ingredients. Though a couple of items are unique to the Korean larder and therefore trickier to find suitable substitution for, but they can easily be found in Korean or Asian grocers and online.

There is a common misconception that Korean cooking is difficult, but I think when we talk about particular cuisines being difficult, it often simply reflects a lack of familiarity. Once we understand the basics, and how the predominant flavours impact and influence one another, we can start building the characteristically robust Korean flavour profiles with confidence.

Typically, the flavours of most Korean dishes can be built around what we call *gazn-yangnyeom*, which loosely translates as 'a balanced assorted seasoning'. It broadly consists of a mixture of spring onion (scallion), garlic, toasted sesame seeds/oil, sugar and salt. These are combined with one or more of the trio of Korean fermented *jang* – *ganjang*, soy sauce; *doenjang*, fermented bean paste; and *gochujang*, fermented chilli paste – to give the dish the desired depth and finish. It really is as simple as a few aromatics combined with an element or two of fermented seasoning.

On English + Korean Names

Losing the ability to speak my mother tongue fluently has been one of the main contributing factors that made me question my identity. I couldn't grasp the language of my birth well enough and felt uncomfortable using it even with my daughter.

Food and stories calling upon my taste memories have been the only medium that I relied on to share with my daughter the wealth of Korean culture I knew. When I came to write this book, it was therefore beyond important to me to strike the balance between the languages, to use them not to alienate the reader – as they had sometimes made me feel alienated from my Korean culture – but to open doors to understanding.

I have therefore included Korean names for each of the recipes, as I wanted the dishes to have the provenance of their origins, to have the roots which are either Korean dishes that I grew up eating or that trace back to the traditional meals that have directly influenced the recipes I have developed for the book. And I wanted the readers, including my daughter, to be able to look up the dishes online for what they are, to extend their exploration.

Beyond that, I have only included other Korean names where they illuminate areas of Korean cuisine or culture, or spotlight my childhood memories. I did not want to force readers to try to cope with unfamiliar words but I did – and do – hope that some words will become familiar – so then I will be a step closer to fulfilling one wish of making *banchan* as recognizable a term as tapas.

| Rice | Koreans mainly eat short-grain white rice, which is very similar to Japanese rice, often labelled sushi rice. When you buy your rice for these recipes, look for Korean or Japanese short-grain rice or sushi rice. You won't get the same results with long-grain rices, such as Jasmine or Basmati, nor with other short-grain rices used in the West, such as short-grain (pudding) rice. |

Dry Seasonings

| *Gochugaru* (Korean Red Pepper Flakes) | Korean red pepper flakes are ground down sundried chillies. The result is smoky with a punchy heat that is laced with subtle sweetness. Coarse flakes are used for making kimchi and general cooking. The finely ground powder is sometimes preferred for soups and stews because it gives the broth a smoother finish and helps to control the overall density. I keep a small jar of finely ground powder (especially recommended for Spicy Pulled Beef Soup – page 105). Just use a pestle and mortar or a spice grinder to make your own. Store it in an airtight container placed somewhere cool and dark. |

When the *gochugaru* starts to warm up in oil, it releases its colour and starts to foam, looking like the bud of a flower blooming.

| Salt | For general cooking, I use sea salt flakes such as Maldon sea salt, which has a lovely texture that can give a pleasing contrast to finish a dish. To season soup dishes, I would recommend grinding the salt down a touch so the flakes dissolve more quickly and you can detect the flavour more accurately. |

For salted water for cooking, I use fine sea salt, and as for kimchi, the best thing is Korean coarse sea salt made especially for salting kimchi, which can be found in Korean supermarkets. Substitute coarse sea salt if it is not available.

Sauces

| Soy Sauce | A vast number of types of soy sauce are traditionally used in Korean homes. Throughout the book, you will find two types of soy sauce: Japanese soy sauce and soup soy sauce. All-purpose Japanese soy sauce is the most similar to more commonly used Korean soy sauce, *jin ganging*. Soup soy sauce is lighter in colour and saltier to taste and is very similar to Chinese light soy sauce, which you can substitute if you cannot find it. |

| *Gochujang* (Korean Chilli Paste) | Korean chilli paste has a subtly smoky undertone with salty sweet umami. It is boldly spicy with complex layers of flavour that I think are unique. The punchy heat of chilli comes from Korean red pepper flakes (*gochugaru*), which is carefully balanced with fermented soybean powder (*meju garu*) and sweet rice syrup made from malted barley powder, sweet glutinous rice flour and salt. The level of spiciness can change quite dramatically depending on what types of chilli is used, so be mindful – brands available on the market will have notes on their heat level. Fortunately, it is one of the most widely available Korean ingredients in the West so it is not a problem that there is no substitute. It keeps well in the fridge. |

Doenjang (Korean Fermented Bean Paste)	Korean fermented bean paste is made from simmered soybeans that are mashed to paste, then shaped like a brick and left to dry outside (usually hung) to ferment for many days. The dried blocks – called *meju* – are then submerged in heavily salted water to break down to form *doenjang* and also *ganjang*, Korean soy sauce. The pungent smell of *doenjang* carries deeply complex flavour profiles that add depth and lingering umami to a dish. It is quite salty and bold. When cooked in water, the smell often reminds me of well-aged Parmesan. You can buy it in Korean or Asian grocers and should store it in the fridge. In the absence of *doenjang*, dark red miso or barley miso can make respectable substitutes.
Yondu (Seasoning Sauce)	This all-purpose liquid vegetable seasoning sauce is a fairly modern addition to the Korean larder. Made from fermented soybeans and concentrated vegetable broth, it is packed full of flavour, and incredibly versatile and impactful. I really like paring it with *doenjang* to season vegetables.

Oils + Liquid Seasonings

Vegetable Oil	For general cooking, I use cold-pressed rapeseed oil or sunflower oil (listed as vegetable oil throughout the book). Extra virgin olive oil is also used for cooking on occasions where vegetables are seasoned simply or for making dressings.
Toasted Sesame Oil	Korean sesame oil is enticingly fragrant with an assertively nutty flavour and aroma. It is widely used in Korean cooking, predominantly as a finishing oil to bring a shot of savoury to the flavour. It pairs especially well with beef and dark greens. Toasted sesame oil has a low smoking point, so be mindful not to let it get too hot when you are cooking.
Perilla Oil	Perilla oil is wonderfully aromatic (an almost cumin like fragrance) and tastes earthy and nutty, nuanced with anise undertones. It is often used to tone down the bitterness in a dish or to neutralize any strong odours associated with fish (see below). It is often favoured for sautéing vegetables, especially the dried types. It is incredibly versatile so I recommend you try it. You'll find it in Korean supermarkets. Once opened, store it in the fridge and try to use it up within a couple of months.
Cheongju (Rice Wine or Sake)	Rice wine has been commonly used in Korean cooking to tenderize meat or fish and to dispel any gamey or fishy odours; the efforts to achieve clean-tasting meat and or fish are evident throughout Korean cuisine. The alcohol evaporates during the cooking process and is believed to carry any smell with it. Koreans use the words *birinnae* or *japnae* to describe a smell or taste that is emitted from fish, raw meat or the blood of animals, regardless of its freshness. An equivalent term does not really exist in Western food culture as most people associate fresh produce with no smell. But Koreans have paid particular attention to removing the delicate smell of live produce. Traditional Korean rice wine, *cheongju*, is not always easy to source so use Japanese cooking sake instead.

Sweet Seasonings

Jocheong (Rice Syrup)

This traditional rice syrup is made by fermenting rice with malted barley powder. It has softer sweetness than sugar, and a faint butterscotch taste with umami undertones. It is typically used in dishes to give a rounded sweetness and also to add shine. *Jocheong* can be found in Korean supermarkets, or look for rice syrup in food stores.

Matsool or Mirin

Sweetened rice wine made for cooking carries a touch of sweetness, gives delicate depth of umami and imparts shine to a dish. Good-quality mirin contains about 14 per cent alcohol which is not mixed with sweetening syrup or vinegar.

Sugar

I think a balanced element of sweetness in seasoning can really highlight the savoury flavours in the same way that a pinch of salt can accentuate the sweetness. Depending on the type of sugar used, it can add rich and complexed undertones to a dish so I use granulated, caster (superfine) and soft brown sugar in the recipes.

Seaweed + Seeds

Dasima (Dried Kelp)

Also known as its Japanese name *kombu*, this is a common ingredient used to make stocks. It has subtly sweet and delicate ocean-like saltiness, and works well with myriad ingredients to layer more complexed flavours. *Dasima* can be found as a folded large sheet or pre-cut into small squares. Stored in an airtight container, it keeps very well in ambient temperatures.

Gim or *Gim Jaban*

Gim is an ingredient that is often overlooked. Mostly eaten as a snack in the West, it is actually a real powerhouse storecupboard ingredient that can add so much flavour to any dish. I like to crumble it into dishes to add its salty-sweet umami flavour. Use liberally as desired. You can find pre-crumbled bags of seaweed in Korean supermarkets or online – just look for *gim jaban*. They usually come in a resealable pouch; once opened, store in the freezer to keep them crisp.

Toasted Sesame Seeds

Both white and black varieties are commonly used in Korean cooking. While whole seeds are used to garnish dishes to add a nutty flavour and a crunchy texture, when seeds are lightly ground down, the broken-down flesh opens up another level of nuttiness that is quite different from the whole seeds. When a recipe calls for lightly crushed or ground sesame seeds, simply crush the whole seeds lightly with a pestle and mortar or spice grinder – you don't want a fine powder.

Other Ingredients

Eggs

The eggs used throughout the book are either organic or free-range, which are often sold in mixed sizes. I select the larger ones for the recipes in this book.

Aromatics

Aromatics, such as garlic and ginger, are peeled, then finely minced to a purée using a knife, micro grater or garlic press, or pounded into a paste using a pestle and mortar. The easiest way to peel ginger is using a teaspoon.

Fresh green chillies used in the book are jalapeño – or serrano if you prefer a mild variety – otherwise finger chillies or bird's eye chillies are used for heat. Fresh red chillies are the long Spanish variety when mild, or bird's eye chillies for heat. Removing the seeds will lessen the heat. Where I specify that the chillies are deseeded, the dish doesn't use the seeds either for heat or aesthetics. If not specified, then it's up to you.

A Few Housekeeping Notes

Whilst cooking Korean food doesn't require any special tools or skills, it involves a fair bit of julienning vegetables. I have found that a decent mandoline – and learning to use it safely – really helps to prepare the vegetables into even slices before cutting into matchstick-thin strips with a knife. Some mandolines have a blade that juliennes in one swipe.

Muslin or cheesecloth appears from time to time, when separating juices from puréed solids, such as fruits and aromatics. It's worth investing in some as it is inexpensive and much better than the next-best alternative of a thin tea towel, which would do the job – just about.

I always find cooking most pleasurable when all the elements are prepped according to the recipe and set out clearly. Please do read through the recipes beforehand to familiarize yourself with the preparation and method and make sure you are fully equipped with everything you need to enjoy the process – there's nothing worse than getting halfway through cooking a dish only to find yourself needing another three hours or three more ingredients to finish the recipe. I've been there!

Korean home cooking is intuitive and versatile. Whilst the methods and ingredients are laid out to guide you through the process, they are suggestions rather than definitive rules. While the timing of all the recipes has been checked over and over again to ensure their accuracy, there are many variable factors that influence them: the type of pan you use, how powerful your oven or hob might be, the way your ingredients are prepped in your kitchen. All these can influence the timing. So I suggest you use the timings as a prompt but mostly rely on your instinctive senses: smell, sound, sight and taste. I hope the recipes are equipped with enough cues for every dish, so you can look out for the signs that they are ready to serve and enjoy.

The Rice Table + Quantities

The rice table is a typical meal table of an ordinary Korean home which consists of rice, soup, a collection of three to five *banchan* dishes, kimchi and a main dish of meat or fish that forms a naturally balanced everyday meal. Rice and soup are served individually but the other dishes are shared amongst the diners. The spread is produce-led and highly seasonal and becomes more elaborate depending on the occasions, such as birthdays or seasonal holidays.

I have given the number of servings that I felt was most appropriate to how you are likely to serve the individual recipes, so some are for two and some are for four, but you can adjust them up or down quite easily to suit the occasion.

Making It Your Own

The dishes here are largely based on the memories of taste from my childhood and likely to reflect my upbringing, but they have also been influenced by the multicultural food scenes I have experienced as an adult in London. I come from Seoul, where food is known to be dainty and seasoned with a light touch. My father carries the delicate palate of Seoul, while my mother's tastes are honest and unadorned with depth that focuses on the essential flavours of ingredients. I like spicy dishes to be bold and vigorous, but not so overpoweringly hot that you can't taste the flavours. I hope the balance of flavours here welcomes you with glowing warmth and deliciousness, but the level of saltiness and spice (as in chilli heat) are a rather subjective thing, so please do taste the dishes as you are cooking and adjust accordingly to ensure the flavours work for you.

Making Friends with Korean Ingredients

Banchan:
The Small Plates

one

banchan is both singular + plural

I thought a lot about the semi-basement flat we once lived in when I was child, and the smell of frying onions. Nothing else was in the pan in my memory as far as I could remember, but both my sister and my mother are adamant that it also had fishcakes in it. Perhaps.

It is entirely possible that what I remember is the beginning of a particular recipe, where gently fried onions provide the backbone of a stir-fried *eomuk* (Stir-Fried Fishcakes with Green Peppers, page 31). But my memories are clear, and only fixated on the deliciously sweet fragrance of soy sauce and onions caramelizing in sugar and butter-soft garlic. I remember my mother's rustic, almost reluctant hands. She sliced the onions on the old wooden chopping board that had definitely seen better days. But the clumpy sound of the blunt knife hitting the board comforted me in the strangest ways.

The small, musty-aired flat was the home where my mother enjoyed her first stand-up kitchen sink, and her brand new two-ring gas hob became her most prized possession that made her life easier.

A small fridge with an even smaller freezer wasn't always full but my mother had a real knack for fruitful cooking that could turn a few small handfuls of radishes into tantalizingly spicy salads. She simmered sweet summer courgettes (zucchini) with salted prawns (shrimp), and made perfectly steamed custardy eggs that had a faint ocean-flavoured saltiness. She was thrifty enough to know that old newspapers were best saved for frying fish. I remember watching her fold up a few sheets of newspaper to form the loosely fitting lid for the top of the pan to soak up all the splutters of oil and smell.

My mother was an inventive cook with good taste and generous hands. She was purposefully frugal, always preserving and fermenting the vegetables in season. Her food was unfussy and had the soul of rural country, heavily influenced by my maternal grandmother's traditional cooking style that belonged to a coastal town. Her small plates of sharing dishes moved fluidly from spring through to winter, and our rice table was small but honest with so much love and respect for the produce in abundance.

We went foraging together in spring to nearby mountains to see the earth awaken with the gift of wild bitter greens. Forest-green mugworts were the taste of my childhood in April, which were transformed into my favourite chewy rice cakes. Summer in the house was flavoured with strawberry jams in jars that lasted until the next autumn, while winter was dedicated to bone broths.

Times were simple and innocent. There were enough twinkling stars in the sky to wish for our dreams, and I had all the time in the world to sit by my mother to watch in awe as she salted cabbage in crockpots to make kimchi. I remember my father digging a hole to bury the earthenware pots beneath the ground late at night for the ceremonial event of family *gimjang* before the first frost in winter. And these are the memories of my ordinary childhood that I miss the most.

-

Banchan – the same word is used for a single dish or a spread of dishes – accompanies every meal and offers a variety of textures and flavours to serve alongside kimchi. When I was growing up, it was often said you could tell how good the cook was by the spread of *banchan* dishes offered. Wherever you go in Korea, you are likely to be welcomed with an array of small plates covering the entire table – our 'rice table' – and that's way before the main event takes centre stage. I think *banchan* is such a unique culture of Korean cuisine and perfectly demonstrates the kind-hearted and generous nature of Korean hospitality.

Notes on Planning + Accessibility

If you are not used to a style of cooking, planning multiple dishes can be a daunting task, but fear not: the majority of these dishes can be prepared in advance and generally keep very well in the fridge for a good few days. In most Korean homes, people batch prepare a few basic dishes that are eaten over the next few days, served with one or two fresh dishes, such as grilled meat, fish, seasonal stew or soup at each meal to keep things interesting.

I have divided this chapter into five sections, grouping dishes by the different cooking techniques so you can reach out with ease to build your own rice table spread that suits your mood and the time you have available. Most dishes in the chapter are straightforward and quick to prepare.

While the most traditional way to enjoy these dishes is in a selection put together at one meal, I've also found that you can serve just one or two dishes with an accompanying bowl of rice or a dish of meat or fish, which can be a more practical way to weave them into your weekly meal plan.

I have carefully chosen the ingredients to contain a variety of widely available vegetables, but do feel free to adapt them to suit your locality, and please experiment with different produce.

On Tossing with Your Hands

The ingredients for tossed salad – *muchim namul* – dishes are best massaged by hand to manipulate not only the flavours but also the texture. Many Koreans believe that the touch of the fingertips can influence the overall harmony of flavour. The term *sonmat* – which literally translates as 'hand taste' – is often used for a good cook who demonstrates exceptional sense of taste through the experience of their hands. And beyond the harmony of the natural diversity of cultures (microflora) that exist on a cook's hands being translated into the dishes, I also think it's the tender love and passion of the cook that ultimately delivers the flavour, which is more intimate as a result.

Sautéed Courgettes

I often think there is a remarkable similarity between Italian and Korean cooking. Both cuisines are led by seasonal produce with emphasis on honest cooking that respects the natural character of each ingredient. This particular dish always reminds me of the way Italians treat their greens: sautéed simply in plenty of good-quality oil with nothing much besides a few garlic cloves and maybe a pinch of flaked chilli. You can really taste the courgettes for what they are, hence the dish is often cooked with young courgettes back home in Korea, to celebrate their wonderful sweetness. The fresh chilli imparts colour rather than heat.

Serves 4

1½ tbsp extra virgin
   olive oil
2 garlic cloves, minced
300g (10½oz) courgettes
   (zucchini), sliced into
   half-moon shapes
¼ onion, thinly sliced
½ tsp sea salt flakes
1 tbsp mirin
½ tsp toasted white
   sesame seeds,
   lightly crushed
½ long mild red
   chilli, deseeded
   and thinly sliced

Put the olive oil and garlic into a cold sauté pan and place it over a medium heat. I like to start the garlic in a cold pan to slowly infuse the flavour into the oil. It will soon start to make a lightly sizzling sound and smell very fragrant but the garlic shouldn't colour.

As soon as it is warmed up to this point, add the courgettes and onions along with the salt. Sauté gently over a low–medium heat for 5 minutes, stirring occasionally and checking that the pan does not look too dry. If it does, add a splash of water, a little at a time so that it doesn't make a puddle.

After 5 minutes, add the mirin and cook for a further 5 minutes or until the courgettes are cooked to your liking. I like mine tender but not completely mushy so there is still a little bite left in them. If you prefer them more stewed down, put a lid on the pan now to steam the courgettes completely. It is entirely up to you.

When the courgettes are cooked to your preference, check for final seasoning and add a touch more salt to taste. Remove from the heat. Stir in the sesame seeds and chilli.

The dish makes a great component for *Bibimbap* (page 166) and can be served both warm or cold. It will keep well for three to four days in the fridge stored in an airtight container.

Sautéed Radish

Korean radish, known as *mu*, is slightly rounder and shorter than the more widely known daikon radish, and tastes mildly spicy with peppery undertones. You can use either for this dish. Spring crops of Korean radish are often used to make radish kimchi as they are still fairly firm and dense, whereas summer crops are considered more watery and rather spicy with a little sweetness, so dishes are often prepared with the addition of sugar to balance the flavour. As the radish season peaks through autumn and early winter, crops harvested around this time are considered the sweetest varieties of all. Winter radish is especially treasured in Korea, as its density lends a refreshingly crunchy bite and almost effervescent sweetness that outweighs its spicy character.

I adore the undeniably simple cooking that champions the humble radish here. When cooked, its mildly spicy character softens into a wonderfully comforting, neutral taste and the firm flesh becomes tender and soothingly sweet. Perilla oil, often used to neutralize any bitterness in cooking, acts to lift the radishes and gives the dish slightly nutty undertones. If you don't have perilla oil, you can substitute the more readily available toasted sesame oil, although it is well worth trying to get hold of perilla oil, which you'll find in Korean or Asian grocers. It has a low smoking point, much like toasted sesame oil, so to compensate for this, I use vegetable oil as carrier oil.

The way radish is cut is especially important in this recipe as radishes sliced against the grain will break down and turn into a mush. It is therefore important that you cut the radishes into 5cm (2in) long pieces first, then slice them thinly lengthways before cutting them into matchsticks

Serves 4

1 tbsp perilla oil
½ tbsp vegetable oil
400g (14oz) Korean radish or daikon radish, julienned
1 tbsp mirin
2 garlic cloves, minced
1–3 tbsp water
1 tsp sea salt flakes
1 spring onion (scallion), minced
1 tsp toasted white sesame seeds

Heat both the perilla and vegetable oils in a sauté pan over a medium heat. Add the radishes along with the mirin and garlic. Cook for 7 minutes, giving it a gentle stir from time to time. If the pan appears a little dry at this point, add a splash of water (about 1–2 tablespoons at a time) to keep it just slightly moist. The radishes will change colour from opaque white to slightly translucent as they cook, and you should be able to smell the nutty aromas of perilla oil as well as the faintly sweet scent of the radishes.

When the radishes have softened, add the salt to season – don't be tempted to add the salt at the beginning as it will draw out too much water. Add another splash of water to continue cooking for 5 minutes until the radishes are tender. Stir in the spring onion and toasted sesame seeds, then cook for a couple more minutes until the spring onion has softened a little but still looks vibrantly green in colour.

The dish makes a great component for *Bibimbap* (page 166) and is delicious warm or cold. It will keep well for up to five days in the fridge stored in an airtight container.

STIR-FRIED

Tofu with Buttered Kimchi

Dubu Kimchi is made up of two parts: poached tofu and stir-fried kimchi. It is a popular dish often served as *anju*, a Korean word that means 'drinking food'. Soured, overripe kimchi is prized for its flavoursome tanginess that works perfectly in stir-fried dishes, often paired with rich, fatty pork to dial down the complex, sour pungency with contrasting richness. The loud and bold flavour of kimchi is warmly supported by simple poached tofu that is welcomingly tender on the tongue. We seek refuge in the barely nutty, almost bland neutral taste, for a relief from the chilli heat.

Sautéed kimchi here is cooked down a little further, with the addition of tomatoes, to the consistency of a thick kimchi sauce. The naturally sweet and sour taste of tomato balances and complements the tangy flavours of kimchi.

Tofu can be steamed, blanched or even lightly pan-fried, if preferred. The recipe uses more readily available firm tofu for accessibility. However, I do like to steam medium-set tofu when I can get hold of it, as the blocks are just about firm enough handle without too much caution and have a wonderfully soft texture that goes really well with the sauce.

Serves 4

1 tbsp vegetable oil
½ onion, thinly sliced
200g (7oz) minced (ground) pork
½ tsp freshly cracked black pepper
20g (¾oz) unsalted butter
2 garlic cloves, minced
350g (12oz) overripe kimchi, roughly chopped
2 tsp golden granulated sugar
1 tbsp mirin
1½ tbsp *gochugaru* (Korean red pepper flakes)
1 tbsp soy sauce
200g (7oz) tinned chopped tomatoes
396g (14oz) block of firm tofu
sea salt flakes

To finish

1 tbsp toasted sesame oil
½ tsp toasted white sesame seeds
1 spring onion (scallion), thinly sliced
a pinch of black sesame seeds

Heat the vegetable oil in a large sauté pan over a medium heat. Add the onion with a pinch of salt and fry for 1–2 minutes to soften. When the onion has collapsed and is starting to smell fragrant, add the pork and the cracked black pepper and stir frequently for about 8–10 minutes until lightly browned, without allowing it to burn. It should be golden brown in colour with an almost sweet, caramelizing smell.

Lower the heat and melt in the butter with the garlic, then add the kimchi, sugar, mirin and *gochugaru*. Give it a good stir to combine the ingredients, then sauté gently for 5 minutes, stirring occasionally. Make sure not to burn the *gochugaru*. We are not here to caramelize the kimchi, rather to soften it slowly in luscious fat.

After 5 minutes, your pan should look a little drier than when you started to fry the kimchi. Stir in the soy sauce, ensuring it is completely incorporated, before adding the tomatoes. Let it simmer for a further 10 minutes.

Meanwhile, bring a pan of well-salted water to the boil. Slice the tofu into two long blocks about 4cm (1½in) wide. Gently drop the tofu blocks into the boiling water and poach them gently for 5 minutes over a low heat. Carefully drain the tofu and cool slightly, taking care of the hot steam. When they're cooled down enough to handle, cut each block into 2cm (¾in) thick slabs.

By now, the kimchi should be ready. Check the seasoning and add a pinch more salt or sugar, if necessary. To finish, stir in the sesame oil and white sesame seeds. Reserve some of the spring onion for garnish, if you like, and add the remainder.

To serve, transfer the sliced tofu slabs onto a serving platter or individual plates, along with the sautéed kimchi either on top or on the side. Finish with the black sesame seeds and reserved spring onion on top.

STIR-FRIED

STIR-FRIED

Stir-Fried Fishcakes with Green Peppers

Eomuk Bokkeum

One of my early memories of food often takes me back to the fishcake cart in a small local market. Near the bus stop was the entrance to the market, which was home to a neat row of general stores selling anything from kitchen wares and haberdashery, to fairly standard clothes shops where my mother often bought cheap bundles of socks or tights. The narrow stretch of useful but somewhat mundane shops eventually faded into the background as we negotiated our way through the narrow alley, allured by the delicious smells and exuberant sounds of life that made my head spin in awe.

The hustle and bustle of tiny food stalls sat in cramped but perfectly orderly fashion amongst the chaos. The loosely covered outdoor market was dimly lit, with shards of light occasionally breaking through the gaps between the thick tarpaulin sheets that roofed us. You could smell anything from salty fermented fish guts to sweet dough frying in sizzling oil as you weaved your way through the crowd, the occasional waft of grease-licked savoury pancakes or steaming bowl of noodles making you hungry. My mother occasionally sat us around the *soondae* stall where an old lady sold her homemade Korean blood sausages accompanied by a selection of offal on the side: usually sliced pig's liver, heart or lung. Other times, we were treated to addictively salty-sweet fishcakes freshly fried at the tiny cart tucked away in the corner.

Korean fishcakes can be found in the freezer section in most Asian grocers. They come in various shapes, from the more common flat, square sheets to round balls – any shape works perfectly fine here. Fishcakes usually have a fair bit of grease on them before cooking, so plunge the frozen fishcakes in just-boiled water for 1 minute, then drain.

The dish will keep well for up to three days, though I think it tastes better warm, hence the small portion size here. Store the leftovers (if you have any) in the fridge in an airtight container. The dish can be served cold or reheated once, either in the microwave or refried with a splash of water.

Heat the vegetable oil in a wok or frying pan (skillet) over a medium heat. Add the onion and stir-fry for a couple of minutes until softened a little. The onion doesn't need to be completely collapsed or caramelized – just soft enough to take away the rawness.

Stir in the green pepper along with the fishcakes and garlic. Continue to stir the pan energetically for 1–2 minutes to stop them from catching on the bottom of the pan. You will notice the fishcakes appear softer and the aroma of the garlic will be released.

Add the mirin and sugar, then stir it around to combine. As the sugar starts to melt and the alcohol in the mirin evaporates, it will smell of caramelizing sugar. Lower the heat and swiftly add the soy sauce, *gochugaru* and black pepper. Give it a good stir and cook for a further 2 minutes until everything is well combined and appears glossy. Remove from the heat and stir in the sesame seeds before serving.

Serves 2

1½ tbsp vegetable oil
½ onion, thinly sliced
½ green (bell) pepper, deseeded and sliced
150g (5oz) Korean fishcakes, cut into bite-sized pieces
2 garlic cloves, minced
2 tbsp mirin
1 tsp golden granulated sugar
1½ tbsp soy sauce
1 tsp *gochugaru* (Korean red pepper flakes)
¼ tsp freshly cracked black pepper
¼ tsp toasted white sesame seeds

King Oyster Mushrooms with *Doenjang* Butter Sauce

Unlike other types of mushroom, beautifully taut king oyster mushrooms have wonderfully dense and meaty stems that hold their shape even after cooking. When cut along the length, they have a pleasantly resistant, slightly chewy texture similar to pulled meat. Cut against the grain, I think they are somewhat reminiscent of a scallop. I love pairing oyster mushrooms with bold, punchy flavours to amplify the rich, savoury taste. The complex umami notes of *doenjang* work a treat, with a generous dose of rich butter helping to melt in the flavour that's sweetened enough to bring out the savouriness.

Dry-frying the mushrooms is particularly important, as it helps to remove some of the moisture and thereby to intensify the mushrooms into meaty morsels packed full of depth of flavour. It's a technique I adapted from observing my mother blanch mushrooms before seasoning.

Serves 2

4 king oyster mushrooms, about 300g (10½oz)
½ tsp sea salt flakes
1 tbsp vegetable oil
2 garlic cloves, minced
2 tbsp mirin
20g (¾oz) unsalted butter
1–2 green finger chillies, sliced
1 tsp toasted white sesame seeds

For the sauce

1 tbsp *doenjang* (Korean fermented bean paste)
1 tsp *yondu* (seasoning sauce)
1 tsp golden granulated sugar
100ml (3½fl oz/scant ½ cup) water

In a small mixing bowl, combine the sauce ingredients. Set aside until needed.

Slice the mushrooms lengthways about 5mm (¼in) thick. Place a large, heavy-based frying pan (skillet) over a medium heat and get it nice and hot. Transfer the sliced mushrooms into the hot pan and sprinkle with the salt. Dry-fry for 5 minutes, turning occasionally to help the mushrooms cook evenly. You should notice the mushrooms start to lose some moisture and become softened and golden in places. Once the mushrooms have collapsed completely, lower the heat and add the vegetable oil and garlic. Briefly sauté to activate the aromas of the garlic – you want to be moving the pan constantly to prevent the garlic from burning.

Swiftly stir in the mirin and cook for 2 minutes. Add the sauce and cook for a further 2 minutes until the mushrooms have absorbed the flavour and there is about 2 tablespoons of liquid left in the pan. Melt in the butter to emulsify into the sauce – it should only take a minute or less. Remove from the heat and stir in the chillies and sesame seeds.

Divide into two bowls and serve warm with plain steamed rice.

Asparagus + Citrus Salad

I have a real thing about tart things laced with sugar and spice, which is hardly surprising given that my mother ate savoury jelly salads made with agar or acorn drenched in sharp vinegar, throughout her entire pregnancy with me, when she was finally able to stomach something other than chewing on a few grains of raw rice. Perhaps it was then, in my mother's womb, that I began to embrace the taste of sour.

Naengchae, which translates as 'cold vegetables or greens', is essentially a cold salad of finely julienned vegetables with or without the addition of meat or fish, and typically dressed with tart and spicy mustard sauce. The dressing here is the shining star and works with a wide range of vegetables – whatever is in season. A decent level of the nose-tingling heat of mustard, which catches at the back of the throat, is considered an important quality of this dish to perk up a tired palate. Use Japanese wasabi paste instead of English mustard if you want to add more of an invigoratingly pungent burst of heat.

The version shared here celebrates the season of asparagus, pairing subtly sweet, earthy green spears with tart citrus, which makes a brilliant accompaniment to LA Short Ribs (page 126).

Whilst *naengchae* may sound like a dish for summer, I actually think the dressing is perfect for adding the vibrant piquancy to any seasonal vegetables all year round. Tart, almost-salty winter tomatoes can brighten the palate with thinly sliced red onion to contrast the texture. Or try tossing barely blanched, crunchy beansprouts with shredded seafood sticks (or squid) and grassy-green peppers or chillies to make an unassumingly invigorating salad.

Serves 2–4

400g (14oz) asparagus
½ tbsp extra virgin
   olive oil
sea salt flakes
1 large orange
   or grapefruit
a few sprigs of mint,
   leaves picked

For the dressing
2 tbsp cider vinegar
2 tbsp water
1 tbsp golden caster
   (superfine) sugar
1 tbsp soup or
   light soy sauce
1½ tsp English mustard

To finish
½ tsp toasted white
   sesame seeds

Place all the ingredients for the dressing in a mixing bowl. Combine well until the sugar has fully dissolved and the mustard is incorporated. Set aside.

Trim off the woody and tough ends of the asparagus. I also like to peel the stalks about 4cm (1½in) away from the bottom so they are aesthetically pleasing, but it is up to you. Coat the trimmed asparagus with olive oil, then chargrill on a hot griddle pan for 2–3 minutes on each side, turning once or twice to char evenly. Once a good char mark appears, add a splash of water to introduce some moisture, so that it almost steams. There is no need to cover. Let it cook for a minute or two to steam through but still retain some bite. Carefully transfer the asparagus onto a shallow, rimmed serving platter, sprinkle with a pinch of sea salt flakes and set aside.

To prepare the citrus, use a sharp knife to top and bottom the fruit – this will give you a solid flat base to work from. Using one smooth downward stroke, cut away the pith and skin of the fruit, following the natural curved shape of the fruit as a guide. Insert the knife between the membranes to segment the fruit – you may reserve the juices that you catch for another use.

Place the segmented fruit and mint in the dressing and combine well. Spoon on top of the asparagus and finish with a sprinkle of toasted sesame seeds and a few drops of olive oil before serving.

Spicy Radish Salad

Korean radish salad can be made in many different ways. Some people say salting the shredded radishes beforehand improves the texture as it removes most of its natural water. I disagree. Unsalted radishes have a refreshing effervescence that is unique to the radish and adds a natural tanginess. I think that salting the radish somehow removes that freshness and makes the radishes chewier and less crunchy. I am here for the sharp, mildly spicy bite.

Fruity *gochugaru* adds a moderate level of heat that balances the sugar. It isn't uncommon to see it dressed with a touch of vinegar to sharpen it up; I don't think it is necessary as it makes the salad rather wet, though it pairs well with carrot, beetroot or kohlrabi – all great vegetables to substitute for the radish.

Please do use a good-quality sesame oil as it works to bind and perfume the dish beautifully right at the end; I think it is the most quintessentially Korean touch.

As with Sautéed Radish (page 26), the way the radish is cut is especially important to retain a good crunchy texture. Cut the radish into 5cm (2in) long pieces first, then slice each piece thinly lengthways before cutting into matchsticks. I like to add the sugar right at the beginning to properly sweeten the radishes. It is often said that seasoning the dishes in the order of sweet, salty, sour and *jang* (the trio of Korean fermented seasoning such as *ganjang*, *doenjang* or *gochujang*) ensures a more harmonious seasoning.

Serves 4

400g (14oz) daikon
  radish, julienned
1 tbsp *gochugaru* (Korean
  red pepper flakes)
1 tbsp golden
  granulated sugar
½ tsp sea salt flakes
2 tsp fish sauce
3 garlic cloves, minced
1 spring onion (scallion),
  minced
1 tsp toasted sesame oil
1 tsp toasted white
  sesame seeds
1 tbsp cider vinegar
  (optional)

Wear some protective gloves when you do this so you can distribute the vibrant red colour of the *gochugaru* through the white radishes, making them a mouthwatering orange-red without your hands ending up the same colour. Place the julienned radishes, *gochugaru* and sugar into a large mixing bowl and gently massage them by hand.

Add the salt, fish sauce, garlic and spring onion. Combine thoroughly with a good grip of the fingertips, pinching and massaging to bring everything together. Check the seasoning and add a pinch more salt, if necessary. Toss in the sesame oil and seeds. Add the vinegar, if using – I don't for the radish.

The dish will keep well for five days in the fridge, stored in an airtight container. You may notice more moisture as it matures in the fridge as the radishes will naturally release their water but it doesn't impair the taste. This makes a great topping for *Bibimbap* (page 166), is excellent with fried egg and makes a lovely accompaniment for grilled meat.

Banchan: The Small Plates

TOSSED + DRESSED

Beansprout Salad – Two Ways

Sukju Namul

Beansprouts, especially soybean sprouts, are one of the most commonly used everyday vegetables in Korea. From simply seasoned salad (always cooked, never raw) to a speedy hangover-curing soup in the morning, it is an easy go-to ingredient that every home cook relies on to whip up something quick on a whim. Even the small, unassuming corner shops used to sell it by the handful, freshly picked from the bucket crowded with sprouts, carefully covered with a dark, fleece-like cloth to stop the heads from turning green.

Whilst soybean sprouts have pronouncedly nutty and crunchy heads with more fibrous stems, I tend to cook this dish with mung beansprouts, as they are more widely available in the UK. Mung beansprouts, when cooked, have a softer texture and taste neutral with an almost refreshing quality to them. You can use either.

These quantities are for four servings of beansprouts with either the stir-fried or the spicy salad. Both will keep well for a couple of days in the fridge, stored in airtight container. They make a great topping for *Bibimbap* (page 166) and an excellent side dish for LA Short Ribs (page 126) or Roasted Pork Belly (page 140).

Bring a pan of salted water to the boil. It is useful to have a bowl of cold water ready close by, so you can plunge the blanched beansprouts immediately into cold water. When the water is rapidly boiling, carefully drop in the beansprouts and blanch them for 3 minutes until a little floppy. Using tongs or a wire skimmer, transfer the beansprouts to the bowl of cold water, then drain. Gently squeeze the water out of the beansprouts as much as you can by hand without squashing them. Put them in a mixing bowl and set aside.

To make the stir-fried salad, put both the vegetable and perilla oils into a cold sauté pan with the garlic and spring onion. Gently heat them up over a medium heat to the point where they start to make a sizzling sound and smell fragrant but are not browned. Add the beansprouts and the *yondu* sauce and sauté for 5 minutes before stirring in the ground sesame seeds. Check for seasoning, adjusting with a pinch of sea salt flakes, if necessary. Serve warm or at room temperature. Store in the fridge once completely cooled.

To make the spicy beansprout salad, add the remaining ingredients to the blanched beansprouts in the mixing bowl. Toss together to combine by hand, massaging gently to distribute the seasoning evenly. Check for seasoning and adjust it with a pinch more sea salt flakes, if necessary. You can serve immediately or store in the fridge to enjoy later.

Serves 4

300g (10½oz) beansprouts
sea salt flakes, to taste

For the Stir-fried Beansprout Salad
1 tbsp vegetable oil
1 tbsp perilla oil
2 garlic cloves, minced
1 spring onion (scallion), thinly sliced
1 tbsp *yondu* (seasoning sauce)
1 tsp toasted white sesame seeds, lightly crushed

For the Spicy Beansprout Salad
1 garlic clove, minced
1 spring onion (scallion), thinly sliced
½ tsp golden granulated sugar
2 tsp *gochugaru* (Korean red pepper flakes)
1 tbsp soy sauce
1 tbsp toasted sesame oil
1 tsp toasted white sesame seeds

Seasoned Spinach Salad

Sigeumchi Namul

Quickly blanched spinach is seasoned with a simple concoction of ground sesame seeds and salty soup soy sauce, with luscious sesame oil to bring it all together. The initial pungent bitterness of the garlic starts to soften into the background of sweet and earthy spinach as you gently massage the ingredients together, transforming the bowl of just a few ingredients into something wonderfully aromatic and moreish in a matter of minutes. It is undeniably simple; though as with all the simple dishes, it is important to pay attention to the few small details – such as removal of excess water and the way the salad is tossed – in order to maximize the flavour.

In Korea, whole mature spinach, with its blushed pink root still attached – which is deliciously sweet and considered more nutritious – is used for this dish, so if you come across some in the local market, don't trim off the root too much. You can make this dish with whatever spinach you can find, but also try it with other leafy vegetables, such as chard, kale or spring greens. Even a wilting lettuce or salad leaves can be revived in cold water before blanching and treating in a similar way – yes, you really can blanch lettuce!

Serves 4

400g (14oz) spinach
2 tsp toasted white
    sesame seeds,
    lightly crushed
1 tsp soup or light
    soy sauce
scant 1 tsp golden
    granulated sugar
scant ½ tsp sea salt flakes
1 garlic clove, minced
1 spring onion (scallion),
    chopped
1 tbsp toasted
    sesame oil

Bring a large pan of salted water to the boil. It is useful to have a bowl of cold water ready, close by, so you can plunge the blanched spinach immediately into the cold water. When the water is rapidly boiling, carefully drop the spinach into the water to blanch until wilted. After about 20 seconds, the leaves should appear floppy. Using tongs or a wire skimmer, transfer to the bowl of cold water.

If you are using a whole spinach, put the root end of the spinach into the boiling water first for 10 seconds before pushing in the leaf end to continue blanching as above.

Swiftly drain the spinach and rinse under cold water a couple of times. Drain completely, then gently squeeze the water out of the spinach as much as you can by hand. This step is important, as properly wrung spinach will soak up the flavour of the seasoning much better. Too much water left in the spinach, and the whole dish will turn out watery and improperly seasoned. Transfer the ball of squeezed spinach onto a chopping board and chop

roughly. Place the chopped spinach into a large mixing bowl and give it a gentle shake to separate the pieces.

Add the remaining ingredients to the bowl and massage gently with your hands to combine, making sure any clumps of spinach are separated. Check for seasoning and add a pinch more salt, if necessary.

Serve as it is. Alternatively, if you are using it as a part of *Bibimbap* (page 166) or Three-Coloured Seaweed Rice Roll (page 169), proceed ahead with the steps in the relevant recipe.

The seasoned salad will keep well for up to three days in the fridge, stored in an airtight container.

TOSSED + DRESSED

Spring Bitter Greens with *Doenjang*

March in Korea marks the season of bitter greens, typically grown wild. You will see every market stall, greengrocers and supermarket aisle filled with arrays of wild bitter greens. It is believed wild spring greens are packed full of nutrients that will encourage the smoother functioning of our bodies after the long, hard slog of a harshly cold winter. It is also widely understood that the subtle bitterness in these wild greens, when seasoned correctly, will awaken your palate.

There are a few widely available green vegetables that carry similar bitter taste profiles to Korean bitter spring greens: kale, watercress, rocket, celery leaves or radish tops. I particularly like Italian puntarelle when they are in season. Green dandelion-like outer leaves can be blanched and soaked in cold water to soften the intense bitterness before seasoning with *doenjang* and wonderfully aromatic perilla oil to complement the astringent flavour; they work brilliantly together to bring the depth and vibrancy that makes your mouth water. The mellower celery-like inner cores are great sliced thinly and dressed raw and sharp with a touch of vinegar to perk them up.

Whisk together all the ingredients for the dressing in a large mixing bowl. Set aside until needed.

Bring a large pan of salted water to the boil. It is useful to have a bowl of cold water ready, close by, so you can plunge the blanched greens immediately into the cold water. When the water is rapidly boiling, carefully drop in your choice of greens to blanch for 2–3 minutes until wilted. Using tongs or a wire skimmer, transfer to the bowl of cold water, then rinse under cold water a couple of times before draining. Gently squeeze the water out of the greens as much as you can by hand without squashing them.

Place the well-wrung greens into the mixing bowl with the dressing. Add the spring onion and sesame seeds along with the vinegar, if using. Gently massage everything together to combine by hand. Check for seasoning and add a pinch more salt or sugar, if necessary.

Serve immediately or store in the fridge. The seasoned salad will keep well for up to three days in the fridge, stored in airtight container.

Serves 2

200g (7oz) bitter green leaves such as celery leaves, watercress, rocket, radish tops or puntarelle
1 spring onion (scallion), chopped
1 tsp toasted white sesame seeds, lightly crushed
1 tbsp cider vinegar (optional)
sea salt flakes, to season

For the dressing
1 tbsp perilla oil
1 tbsp *yondu* (seasoning sauce) or light soy sauce
2 tsp *doenjang* (Korean fermented bean paste)
½ tsp *gochugaru* (Korean red pepper flakes)
½ tsp golden granulated sugar
1 garlic clove, minced

Mung Bean Pancake

Mung bean pancake, often found in food markets in South Korea, is a particularly well-known dish that has its roots in North Korea. It is said that a true northern-style (*ibuksig*) pancake is shaped thick and large and almost deep-fried in a pool of rendered pork fat, which results in a deliciously nutty and moist pancake with a crispy exterior. This particular mouthfeel of food – often abbreviated to *geotba sogchok*, meaning 'crispy on the outside and moist and juicy inside' – is a valued quality of well-made *bindaettoek*, which can be achieved when you have a harmony of three elements: a batter with correct consistency, good heat control and the right amount of fat. Seoul-style pancakes are often shaped much smaller with decorative details such as diagonally sliced red chillies on top.

Traditionally, mung beans are soaked and washed to remove the green outer skin. If there is too much skin in the batter, the texture of the pancake becomes tough. From cooking Indian dal, I learnt that moong dal is a split mung bean without the husk, which makes it an ideal time-saving swap. I soak them for as little as an hour to soften, then proceed as usual. Refrigerate or freeze any leftover pancakes – to reheat, refry them from room temperature in a little oil to revive their crispiness.

The dish is best served with Soy Sauce Pickled Onions (page 88): the sharp, sweet and salty pickling juice works perfectly as a dipping sauce. If you don't have pickled onions handy, try it with Chive Dipping Sauce (page 222).

Makes about four 15cm (6in) diameter pancakes

200g (7oz/1 cup) moong dal
3 tbsp white short-grain rice
200g (7oz) minced (ground) pork, preferably 20% fat
2 garlic cloves, finely minced
1 tbsp soy sauce
2 tsp mirin
1 tsp toasted sesame oil + 1 tbsp for the batter
¼ tsp freshly cracked black pepper
100g (3½oz) mung beansprouts
100g (3½oz) drained ripe kimchi (Cut Cabbage Kimchi, page 75), roughly chopped
2 spring onions (scallions), chopped
½ tsp sea salt flakes
vegetable oil, for frying

Put the moong dal and rice in a large bowl and fill with enough cold water to cover. Leave to soak for at least 1 hour or overnight. Rinse a couple of times, then drain completely. Set aside.

Place the minced pork in a small mixing bowl with the garlic, soy sauce, mirin, a teaspoon of sesame oil and the black pepper. Combine and set aside.

Bring a pan of salted water to the boil. It is useful to have a bowl of cold water ready, close by, so you can plunge the blanched beansprouts into the cold water. When the water is boiling rapidly, drop in the beansprouts and blanch them for 2 minutes until floppy. Using tongs, transfer to the bowl of cold water and rinse under cold water a couple of times before draining. Gently squeeze the water out of the beansprouts as much as you can by hand, without squashing them. Set aside.

Using a high-speed blender or stick blender, blend the drained, soaked moong dal and rice with 200ml (7fl oz/scant 1 cup) of water until relatively smooth but with a slightly grainy texture. Check by rubbing the blended mixture between your fingertips to see if it feels a little pulpy – if yes, great.

Pour the dal and rice into a large mixing bowl, add the seasoned pork, blanched beansprouts, kimchi and spring onions. Add the tablespoon of sesame oil and the salt. Give it a stir to combine everything into a smooth batter. It should feel like a thick yogurt with bits.

Fill a large frying pan (skillet) with oil to about 5mm (¼in) deep. Place it over a medium heat. When the oil is hot, carefully ladle the batter into the centre of the pan – you should hear a sizzling sound when the batter hits the pan. Spread the batter to make a pancake about 1cm (½in) thick and slightly bigger than the size of a hand. You can adjust the size and thickness but keep in mind that these pancakes can be tricky to flip if they are too big.

Leave the pancake to fry on one side for about 2 minutes on a low–medium heat, while ladling the hot oil to drench over the top of the pancake. You should notice the edges start to crisp up and everything will begin smelling deliciously nutty. Carefully flip the pancake, then continue cooking for a further 2 minutes, or until everything is wonderfully deep golden. Continue working through the rest of batter.

Serve immediately straight out of the frying pan with a side of pickled onions.

Spring Onion Pancake

In Korea, people often say 'a rainy day calls for Korean savoury pancakes (*buchimgae*) and rice wine (*makgeolli*). Many believe that eating crispy, shallow-fried savoury pancakes dipped in a vinegary dipping sauce has a real mood-lifting effect on a dreary, wet day. Some say the sizzling sound of cold pancake batter hitting the hot oil and frying resembles the pitter-pattering sound of raindrops hitting the ground and the whistling wind, hence we subconsciously crave them.

The word *gsohada*, which describes food that smells or tastes nutty, is often used for well-made pancakes, as freshly fried, golden pancakes are aromatic and savoury. The mouthwatering nutty aroma of pancakes translates perfectly into the delicately crispy batter, while the deep umami of charred spring onions really hits the high notes when saturated in salty, sweet, vinegary dipping sauce.

Tapioca flour yields a light and airy batter that is similar to premixed pancake flour used by many Korean home cooks. It is a good versatile basic batter, so do try it with different fillings, such as chopped kimchi, shredded sweet courgettes (zucchini) or odds and ends of vegetables that need using up. I found the texture of the batter improves with an overnight rest in the fridge, as the gluten relaxes, but if you are short on time, resting the batter for 30 minutes will do. The basic batter will last up to three days in the fridge, stored in an airtight container.

Makes three 19cm (7½in) pancakes

3 bunches of spring onions (scallions), about 350g (12oz)
100g (3½oz) squid, cleaned and sliced into small bite-size pieces (optional)
50g (1¾oz) prawns (shrimp), roughly chopped (optional)
1 long mild red chilli, sliced diagonally
2 eggs, lightly whisked
vegetable oil, for frying

For the batter
150g (5oz/scant 1¼ cups) plain (all-purpose) flour
50g (1¾oz/heaped ⅓ cup) tapioca flour
2 tbsp cornflour (cornstarch)
½ tsp sea salt flakes
¼ tsp baking powder
250ml (8½fl oz/1 cup) fridge-cold water

Serve with Chive Dipping Sauce (page 222) or Soy Sauce Pickled Onions (page 88)

Combine all the dry ingredients for the batter in a large mixing bowl. Add the cold water and whisk until smooth, then chill to rest the batter overnight or for 30 minutes, if rushed. The batter might seem thin but it will thicken as the flour swells while it is resting.

Trim the spring onions so they will fit comfortably lengthways in a large frying pan (skillet). Cut any large ones in half lengthways, too, so that they are all a similar thickness. Combine the squid and prawns, if using, in a bowl so you can easily reach out to scatter them onto the pancake. Have all the components ready, as assembling the pancakes will require your attention at certain stages.

Heat 2 tablespoons of oil in the frying pan over a medium heat. Lay one-third of the spring onions in a single layer, without large gaps in between. Ladle one-third of the batter onto the spring onions, spreading to fill any gaps. You will notice a soft whistling sound when the cold batter hits the pan.

Scatter with one-third of the seafood, if using, and the red chillies. Drizzle one-third of the egg on top.

Maintain a medium heat. If the heat is too low, the pancake will soak up too much grease. Listen to the gentle sizzling and notice the consistent bubbles around the edge of the pancake – these are good signs. Soon, the edge of the pancake will start to crisp up. You may need to add a touch more oil around the edge of the pan if it appears a little dry. After 3–4 minutes, dry patches on the top of the pancake will indicate that it is almost cooked. Drizzle a little more oil on top then flip the pancake. Press the centre to help the ingredients settle. Cook for a further 3 minutes or until cooked through and golden. Repeat to make the remaining pancakes.

Serve immediately with dipping sauce and a pair of scissors to cut the pancakes. Leftover pancakes can be stored in the fridge then reheated from room temperature in a hot pan with a little oil to crisp them up.

Pork + Tofu Meatballs

These lesser-known Korean meatballs were often one of the highlights of big gatherings such as *Chuseok* (the Korean mid-autumn harvest festival) and *Seollal* (lunar new year) in my family. No holidays were complete without the day-long event of shaping and dredging the meat, fish and vegetables. Everyone sitting cosily on the floor, centred around the same old electric frying pan that appeared for every seasonal event of the year, we all dutifully took our designated positions in the communal activity of cooking for the occasion.

I came across online that the official name for these meatballs is *donjeonya*: *don* meaning an 'old coin' and *jeonya* meaning 'a dish of dredged minced fish or meat fried in a hot pan with a little oil'. It is an unusual term for me, as I grew up knowing this dish as *dong-gue-rang-ttaeng*, as many other Koreans do. *Dongguerang* loosely translates as 'round' or 'circular' and *ttaeng* is a word that describes the sound of a coin dropping. Given the name, it is not difficult to figure that these meatballs are little round things made with minced pork and tofu.

They are great served with rice or as a beer snack. I like to shape them into rounds but slightly flattened so they are somewhere between the shape of a meatball and a patty, like a well-fluffed velvet pouffe. The gently flattened shape ensures the meat cooks evenly without drying out.

Leftovers will keep well for three days in the fridge, stored in an airtight container, or a couple of months in the freezer.

**Makes about 18
golf-ball-sized patties**

300g (10½oz) minced
   (ground) pork
1 tsp soy sauce
1 tsp mirin
¼ tsp grated ginger root
¼ tsp freshly cracked
   black pepper
about 40g (1½oz) onion
about 40g (1½oz) carrot
1 mild green chilli
1 long mild red chilli
150g (5oz) firm tofu
2 garlic cloves, minced
1 tbsp potato flour
   (starch)
1 tbsp toasted sesame oil
1 tbsp oyster sauce
½ tsp sea salt flakes,
   or to taste
1 tbsp plain (all-purpose)
   flour, for dredging
1 egg, lightly whisked
about 2 tbsp vegetable
   oil, for frying

Serve with Chive Dipping
   Sauce (page 222) or
   Soy Sauce Pickled
   Onions (page 88)

Place the pork in a mixing bowl large enough to accommodate all the ingredients. Season the meat with the soy sauce, mirin, ginger and black pepper. Set aside while you prepare the onion, carrot and both chillies, mincing them as finely as possible so that everything cooks evenly until it is tender with no unwelcome rawness. Mix the minced vegetables with the pork.

Wrap the block of tofu in a piece of muslin or cheesecloth and wring it as tightly as you can to remove the excess water. The tofu inside will crumble as you squeeze and twist, and this is perfectly fine. Carefully transfer the crumbled tofu into the bowl with the pork and vegetables.

Line a baking tray with parchment paper and have it handy so you can put the shaped patties on it as you make them.

Add the garlic, potato flour, sesame oil, oyster sauce and sea salt to the pork and tofu mix. Work the mixture energetically with your hands to combine, as if you are kneading dough, scraping the edges in a scooping motion to thoroughly mix everything together. As you work the mixture, it will start to strengthen and will feel almost sticky.

The amount of salt added here is right for me. However, it might be a good idea to try the seasoning by test-frying a teaspoonful of the mixture before you start shaping the meatballs, so that you can be sure it is right for you. Adjust it accordingly, then start shaping the mixture into small golf-ball-sized patties, pressed gently to flatten into discs measuring about 4–5cm (1½–2in) in diameter. You should finish with about 18 patties.

PAN-FRIED, GRILLED + ROASTED

Put the flour in a tray or shallow, rimmed bowl and carefully roll the patties to lightly dust them. Whisk the egg in a bowl with a pinch of salt.

Set up your cooking station, as you will be dipping and frying at the same time, so you need a row of dusted meatballs, egg, frying pan and a tray or plate lined with kitchen paper so that you can swiftly transfer the cooked meatballs.

Heat the vegetable oil in a frying pan (skillet) over a low–medium heat. Dip a meatball patty in egg, ensuring it is coated evenly so that you don't see the flour, then carefully place in the frying pan at the one o'clock position (imagining the frying pan was a clock face) and cook for 3–4 minutes on each side until cooked through and deliciously golden, then transfer to the prepared plate. At the same time, keep adding meatballs to the frying pan and turning them over, working round the clock face so you know which ones to turn first and which to remove from the pan.

Serve warm or cold with a dipping sauce on the side.

PAN-FRIED, GRILLED + ROASTED

Rolled Omelette with Seaweed

Gyeranmari

In Korea, softly beaten eggs are stuffed with anything from minced vegetables to melting cheese, then rolled into a fluffy log of beautifully scrambled layers. There is no hint of heavy 'eggy-ness', but delightfully light and silky egg that works particularly well with a squirt of tomato ketchup. I like the simplicity and ease of this recipe that delivers a sustaining meal on a whim: be it breakfast, a quick lunch or a cheap, fuss-free dinner.

More traditionally, common choices of filling were sheets of seaweed (like the ones for making sushi) or finely minced carrots and spring onions, but I think pretty much anything goes – I have seen people use salted pollock roe, leftover rice or even frankfurters!

You don't necessarily need a square pan for this but I do find it slightly easier. I use a fairly inexpensive (and very old) non-stick frying pan which is dedicated to making *gyeranmari*. You want to maintain a gentle heat throughout so that the eggs don't overcook. I found using two spatulas really helps to manoeuvre the eggs when folding, especially when cooking in an ordinary round pan. It does take a little practice to get comfortable with what's going on, but you will soon get used to it. Just be a little patient and don't let the first few tears and rips bother you, as in the end, it will all be just fine and taste great!

Crack the eggs into a large jug with a pouring spout and energetically beat to create smooth strands with no lumps. Whisk in the olive oil, mirin, salt and soy sauce, ensuring everything is incorporated. Stir in the onion.

The next step will require your full attention so have the tools you need close by, as well as the whisked egg mixture and a sheet of seaweed. It would be useful to have a chopping board ready so you can transfer the finished roll as soon as it's done.

Heat the vegetable oil in a non-stick frying pan (skillet) over a low heat and swirl it round to coat the pan evenly. You don't need lots of oil but the pan should be well coated. When the oil has warmed up, give the egg mixture a quick stir and pour half of the mixture into the pan. Give the pan a gentle swirl to spread the egg to cover the entire pan. Watch carefully and notice as the edge starts to cook. The middle will look raw in some places and almost barely set in some other patches.

Lay the sheet of seaweed on top, gently pushing it onto the egg. Working from the most-cooked edge, begin rolling up the egg. Do this holding two spatulas at the same time – one to fold and the other to support. Continue rolling up until you get to just over halfway. At this point, the eggs in the pan should have cooked enough for you to bring them closer to you. Add a touch more oil if the pan is looking dry. Pour in half the remaining egg mixture to fill the pan, then continue folding. Repeat again when you're near to the end, pushing the rolled eggs to one side and pouring in the remaining eggs to fill the pan.

Once you have finished folding, it will look like a log. Using the spatulas, gently squeeze the edges to sharpen the shape. If you feel comfortable, flip and turn to firm up all sides. I like mine cooked golden yellow with no browning to ensure a fluffy omelette. Remove from the heat as soon as it's done and transfer to a chopping board. Let it cool for a minute or two before slicing into 2cm (¾in) thick pieces to serve.

Serves 2

4 eggs
1 tbsp extra virgin olive oil
1 tbsp mirin
½ tsp sea salt flakes
½ tsp soup or light soy sauce
1 spring onion (scallion), chopped
1 large sheet of seaweed
1 tbsp vegetable oil, for frying

Serve with tomato ketchup (catsup)

Charred Cabbage in Warm *Gochujang* Vinaigrette

I always think it's a pity that so many people consider cooked cabbage rather unpalatable. In Korea, white cabbage is one of the most commonly used everyday vegetables and everyone loves it. We take advantage of the versatile nature of this humble brassica in every possible way you can imagine. I have certainly grown up eating a lot of cabbage and have a real soft spot for it. When cooked, the crunchy opaque leaves, tightly nestled together, unfurl and turn translucent. The fibrous texture of the raw ingredient softens and becomes tender, unveiling the delicate vegetal nuances that cling onto the bolder flavours, delivering comfort that eats softly on the tongue and gently on the stomach.

This inspiration certainly comes from the contrasting explosion of flavour combinations I experienced as a child – steamed cabbages dipped in tart and sweet *gochujang* dressing – which I have come to appreciate more as a grown up. Slightly charred cabbages boast intensely caramelized sweetness that sits on the verge of bitterness (in a nice way) and pairs well with a warm, garlic acidity laced with smoky *gochujang*.

Eat this with a crispy fried egg on the side and steamed rice to make it a midweek-friendly dinner.

Serves 2–4

½ white cabbage
1 tbsp vegetable oil
½ tsp sea salt flakes
¼ tsp freshly cracked
  black pepper
2 tsp golden granulated
  sugar
2 tsp soy sauce
2 tsp *gochujang* (Korean
  fermented chilli paste)
½ tsp *gochugaru* (Korean
  red pepper flakes)
2 tbsp extra virgin olive oil
2 garlic cloves, minced
2 tbsp cider vinegar

Prepare the cabbage by removing any wilted outer leaves. Slice the cabbage in half lengthways so you have two wedges. Remove the cores and tear the leaves into large, bite-sized pieces. The edges of the pieces will appear uneven and that is perfectly fine. Transfer the torn cabbage to a large mixing bowl and soak it in cold water for 10 minutes. Drain well.

Toss the cabbage with the vegetable oil, salt and black pepper.

Preheat the grill (broiler) to high and place a large empty baking tray under the grill to heat up.

Carefully remove the hot tray from the oven and place the seasoned cabbage onto it. You should notice the sizzling sound as the cold cabbage hits the scorching hot tray. Grill for 7 minutes, turning once or twice to ensure you have an even char. You should notice the edges catching in places. The inside of the cabbage will soften but still retain some bite. When ready, set aside.

Meanwhile, combine the sugar, soy sauce, *gochujang* and *gochugaru* in a small mixing bowl. Give it a good stir and set aside. Put the olive oil and garlic into a small, cold saucepan. Gently warm up over a low heat for a couple of minutes to infuse. I start the pan from cold to prevent the garlic from burning too quickly, so be patient and keep the heat on very low. After 2 minutes or so, you should notice the garlic begin to smell fragrant. Add the soy sauce and *gochujang* mixture to the pan, stirring continuously to incorporate it into the oil. Continue cooking on low for 2 minutes.

Whisk in the cider vinegar and bring it to a warm temperature without boiling. It should only take about 30 seconds. Remove from the heat and set aside.

In a large mixing bowl, combine the cabbage and warm *gochujang* vinaigrette. Serve warm or cold. Stored in an airtight container, it will keep well for a few days in the fridge.

Soy Sauce Glazed Aubergines

Gaji Gangjeong

My mother's rice table in the height of summer celebrated the abundance of long and thin Korean aubergines. Their deep purple skin shined bright even when it was cooked and the firm white flesh always tasted sweet, without a hint of bitterness. Often stir-fried or steamed, my mother's aubergines retained a beautiful thin skin with a delicate chewy texture.

More commonly found Western aubergines tend to be larger and have thicker skin with spongier flesh; frying the aubergines will help to soften the tougher exterior.

Don't cut the aubergines too small as, once salted and squeezed, they will lose some volume. Salting of the aubergines here isn't to remove any bitterness but to remove the excess moisture in order to achieve the right texture. It also prevents the aubergines from getting completely soaked in oil when frying.

Serves 4

For the aubergines (eggplants)

2 aubergines, about 600g (1lb 5oz), quartered lengthways and cut into large bite-size chunks
½ tsp sea salt flakes
3 tbsp potato flour (starch)
vegetable oil, for frying

For the glaze

3 tbsp water
2 tbsp mirin
2 tbsp soy sauce
1 tbsp *jocheong* (Korean rice syrup)
1 tbsp cider vinegar
2 tsp golden granulated sugar
½ tsp freshly cracked black pepper
2 garlic cloves, minced
1 mild red chilli, finely chopped

To finish

½ tsp toasted white sesame seeds
20g (¾oz) toasted peanuts, roughly chopped

Prepare the aubergines by removing the tops. Quarter them lengthways, then cut each quartered pieces into large bite-sized chunks. Transfer the cut aubergines into a colander and combine well with the salt. Place the colander over the bowl or sink and let it sit for 30 minutes then, without rinsing, gently squeeze the aubergines to extract the moisture.

Meanwhile, combine all the ingredients for the glaze in a bowl. Set aside.

Put the potato flour in a bowl or large reusable plastic bag. Add the salted aubergines and coat them generously by tossing or shaking with the top sealed, if you're using the bag. Let it sit for a couple of minutes.

Prepare a cooling rack set over a roasting tray.

Fill a large, heavy-based saucepan with vegetable oil deep enough to submerge the aubergines but not fill the pan more than three-quarters full. Heat the oil to 180–185°C (356–365°F).

Gently lower a few of the aubergine pieces into the oil so they have plenty of room to fry and don't reduce the oil temperature too much. Fry for 3 minutes until they are golden and crispy on all sides. Transfer them onto the cooling rack – I found a wired rack much more effective, as fried aubergines resting on kitchen paper tend to stick. Continue to cook in batches.

Put the glaze mix into a large sauté pan or wok over a high heat and bring to a rapid boil. Cook for about 2 minutes until the sauce has thickened to a loose syrup consistency. Toss in the fried aubergines to coat them evenly with the glaze. Cook for a further minute until the aubergines appear very glossy; you should also have a little bit of sauce left in the pan.

To serve, stir in the sesame seeds and chopped peanuts. Eat immediately while still warm.

DEEP-FRIED

DEEP-FRIED

Sweet + Sour Tofu

Dubu Tangsu

Tangsuyuk is one of many quintessential Korean Chinese dishes, which typically uses lean strips of pork. Dredged in starchy batter, the meat yields an undeniably crispy exterior that doesn't go sweaty, even when doused in velvety sweet and sour sauce. I am opting for tofu here as I always tend to have a block sitting in the fridge, which makes it a great meat-free weeknight dinner.

It is said that these hybrid dishes – known as *junghwa yori* – were developed by Chinese immigrants during the late 19th century, who had to adapt their familiar ingredients and flavours to suit the locality and Korean palate. Some of these dishes have evolved a long way since their beginnings and perhaps now show very little resemblance to the originals, although in essence they remain respectful to their roots.

I think Korean Chinese cuisine really supports my belief that food continues to travel and evolve with people, influencing and educating others to broaden their cultural experiences. We practise our food traditions to remain connected to our heritage and thus to ensure that it lives on through many generations to come.

Pat the tofu dry with kitchen paper, then cut into 2.5cm (1in) cubes. It is easy to do this by cutting the tofu in half down the middle, then quartering each block again before finally cutting them into cubes. Lay the tofu cubes on a tray lined with a sheet of kitchen paper to soak up excess moisture. Salt them generously and leave to stand for 10 minutes.

Meanwhile, combine the sugar, cider vinegar, ketchup, soy sauce, ginger and water in a small mixing bowl. Set aside.

Put the potato flour and cornflour in a bowl or large reusable plastic bag. Add the salted tofu cubes and coat them by tossing or shaking with the top sealed, if you're using the bag. Let it sit for a couple of minutes.

Prepare a cooling rack set over a roasting tray.

Fill a large, heavy-based saucepan with vegetable oil deep enough to submerge the tofu but do not fill the pan more than three-quarters full.

Heat the oil to 175°C (347°F). Gently lower a few of the tofu pieces into the oil so they have plenty of room to fry and don't reduce the oil temperature too much. Fry for 5 minutes until they are evenly golden and crisp on all sides. Transfer them onto the cooling rack. Continue to cook in batches.

Put the prepared sauce mixture in a wok and bring it up to a rapid boil over a high heat. You will notice large bubbles gathering on the surface. Continue to boil for about 3 minutes so the sauce reduces down and thickens slightly. Add the sliced lemon and the pinch of cinnamon.

Reduce the heat. Combine the water and potato flour to make a slurry, then gradually add to the sauce (about two-thirds of it to start with) until it is shiny and the consistency of clear honey. You may not need all the slurry.

Once the sauce has thickened to the desired consistency, toss in the fried tofu and stir to coat. Scatter with the black sesame seeds and serve immediately while warm.

Serves 2

396g (14oz) block of tofu
fine sea salt
3 tbsp potato flour (starch)
2 tbsp cornflour (cornstarch)
vegetable oil, for frying

For the sauce
2 tbsp golden granulated sugar
2 tbsp cider vinegar
1 tbsp tomato ketchup (catsup)
1 tbsp soy sauce
1 tsp grated ginger root
150ml (5fl oz/scant ⅔ cup) water
½ lemon, sliced
a pinch of ground cinnamon, to taste
1 tbsp water
1 tsp potato flour (starch)

To finish
½ tsp toasted black sesame seeds

Mixed Vegetable Fritters

Growing up in Seoul, long school summer holidays came without much help of childcare for my parents. Both of my siblings and I often spent our days at my parents' work, running around their warehouse where a small rest room made a den. We made our own games to entertain ourselves all day long and ran riot in our own little kingdom! Occasionally, my mother asked us to help out with a few small jobs to keep us occupied and under control. In return, we sweetly negotiated deals by requesting takeaways from the local street food vendors where varieties of deep-fried snacks were on offer. At other times, we hid between the boxes and ate obscene amounts of crisps and ice lollies with not a care in the world. And those hot summer days of early morning breeze and sleepy rides home full of fast-moving neon lights at the back of my parents' car, despite what it might sound like, felt intensely free and loving, peppered with tender memories of deliciously nostalgic plates of food that still bring me so much joy.

Naturally sweet root vegetables coated in gorgeously nutty and crispy batter taste friendly and texturally satisfying: it's crunchy on first bite with a lingering softness that hugs the mouth with familiar flavours of everyday vegetables. Although it is more common to use a thick pancake-like batter for this, I much prefer mine with a thin coat of slurry to give the vegetables a chance to show off their flavours. It's a versatile batter, so feel free to add or substitute any odds and ends of vegetables that might need using up.

**Makes 12–16
small fritters**

200g (7oz) sweet
potatoes, julienned
into thin matchsticks
75g (2½oz) carrot,
julienned into thin
matchsticks
½ onion, thinly sliced
vegetable oil, for frying

For the batter
60g (2oz/¼ cup) plain
(all-purpose) flour
15g (½oz/2 tbsp) cornflour
(cornstarch)
½ tsp sea salt flakes
¼ tsp baking powder
½ tsp toasted sesame oil
100ml (3½fl oz/scant
⅓ cup) cold water

Serve with Chive Dipping
Sauce (page 222) or
Soy Sauce Pickled
Onions (page 88)

Place the sweet potatoes in a bowl, cover with cold water and leave to soak for 10 minutes to remove excess starch; you will also want to do this if you are using potatoes. Drain completely and pat dry with a tea towel. Toss together with the carrot and onion. Set aside.

In a large mixing bowl, combine all the ingredients for the batter. Whisk well. Don't worry if the batter seems too runny – that is perfectly fine. Rest the batter in the fridge for 10 minutes.

Toss the vegetables in the batter to coat evenly. The mixture will feel like it won't hold together but, don't worry, that really is perfect.

Prepare a cooling rack set over a roasting tray.

Fill a large, heavy-based saucepan with vegetable oil deep enough to submerge the fritters but do not fill the pan more than three-quarters full. Heat the oil to 175°C (347°F).

Using two spoons, scoop a spoonful of the mixture and carefully slide it into the oil. Let it fry without disturbing it. Though it might look like it is not going to hold its shape, as it cooks, it'll stick together. Don't worry too much about even shapes. They will all be just as delicious. Fry for 3–5 minutes until cooked through and golden with crispy edges. When they are done, transfer them onto the cooling rack. You may have to work in batches to make sure you don't overcrowd the pan.

Serve warm with your choice of dipping sauce.

DEEP-FRIED

Old-School Pork Cutlet

I still remember so vividly the first time I tried this sweet-crumbed, crispy pork cutlet: I was sitting at the high countertop looking into the open kitchen, the warm pot of watery soup was gently bubbling away while the endless slabs of pork were being deep-fried right in front of my eyes. Young families sat in an orderly but crowded fashion and the restaurant was buzzing from the living and breathing sound of excited diners chattering. There, the chefs moved like dancers to the beautifully orchestrated symphony of a working kitchen. Everything felt so electric, and to my young eyes, beyond food, it was magical to be part of something entirely new.

A plate of gigantic slabs of crunchy crisp-fried pork came blanketed under the thick, rich brown sauce – loosely based on demi-glace sauce – and had a perfect touch of acidity that made the pork eat better. It was always served as whole, never sliced, as we were here to eat Western-style food, known as *gyeongyangsik*, with a knife and fork. Cold macaroni salad, which I'd never seen before, shared the same plate, plonked next to shredded cabbages swirled with vinegary ketchup and mayonnaise. And sitting snugly in the middle of all these new things, some perfectly bowled rice and pickled radish made everything a little less foreign.

This old-school pork cutlet, also known by the Japanese name *tonkatsu*, was first introduced to Korea during the Japanese occupation and is believed to trace its roots right back to Europe: think Italian veal Milanese, French escalope or German schnitzel, to name just a few.

While Japanese-style *tonkatsu* in Korea was, and remains, thick and always served sliced, Korean iterations take thinner slices of lean pork, typically cut from the loin. Pork prepared by butchers is flattened and tenderized by being passed through a machine that indents the flesh, leaving the iconic, uniformed lines of marks which prevents the meat from curling.

I like to use a meat mallet to flatten the pork and a needle-bladed meat tenderizer to achieve a similar effect. You can use a rolling pin or the back of the knife to flatten and tenderize but if neither is available to you, just make sure you make a few small cuts to stop the meat from curling when fried.

Serves 2

two 150g (5oz) trimmed
    pork loin steaks
½ onion, roughly chopped
3 tbsp full-fat milk
½ tsp garlic powder
½ tsp sea salt flakes
3 tbsp plain (all-purpose)
    flour
1 egg, whisked with a
    pinch of salt
100g (3½oz/2 cups) panko
    breadcrumbs
vegetable oil, for frying

Prepare the pork slices by flattening and tenderizing with any of my chosen tools (see intro), so the slices are about 1cm (¾in) thick. Use clingfilm (plastic wrap) or a reusable bag to protect the flesh of the pork when flattening. Work through both pieces.

Place the onion and milk in a food processor and blend until smooth. Stir in the garlic powder and salt. Pour over the tenderized pork and refrigerate for 30 minutes.

Meanwhile, combine the sugar, ketchup, Worcestershire sauce, soy sauce and English mustard in a bowl. Mix well and set aside.

Continuing with the sauce, melt the butter in a heavy-based saucepan and add the flour. Cook the flour over a low–medium heat for 3–4 minutes, stirring constantly, until the mixture turns toffee brown in colour, making sure you don't let it burn.

DEEP-FRIED

For the sauce

1 tbsp golden
   granulated sugar
2 tbsp tomato
   ketchup (catsup)
2 tbsp Worcestershire
   sauce
2 tsp soy sauce
1 tsp English mustard
10g (1 tbsp)
   unsalted butter
10g (2 tbsp) plain
   (all-purpose) flour
300ml (10fl oz/1¼ cups)
   water
½ tsp freshly cracked
   black pepper
3 tbsp full-fat milk
sea salt flakes, to taste

To finish

120g (4oz) white cabbage,
   shredded
generous splash of
   Worcestershire sauce
generous splash of extra
   virgin olive oil
good pinch of salt
   and pepper

Carefully pour in the water a little at a time, whisking constantly to keep it smooth. Add the ketchup mixture to the pan and season with the black pepper. Combine well and simmer gently for about 15 minutes to reduce, stirring occasionally.

Stir in the milk and season with a pinch of salt, if necessary. Simmer for 5 minutes to thicken slightly – the sauce should have a pourable consistency. Keep warm until needed.

Remove the pork from the fridge. Scrape off as much of the marinade as possible and pat the meat dry with kitchen paper. Have three shallow, rimmed plates or trays ready: one filled with the flour, one with the eggs and one with the panko breadcrumbs. Spray the breadcrumbs with a little water to moisten.

Keep one hand for the egg and the other for handling the dry ingredients. Lightly dust the pork with flour, dip into the whisked egg, then push into the breadcrumbs gently but firmly until evenly coated. Repeat with the other piece and set aside.

Prepare a cooling rack set over a roasting tray.

Fill a large, heavy-based saucepan or large frying pan (skillet) suitable for deep-frying with vegetable oil. Ideally, it should be filled deep enough to submerge the pork cutlets, but if not, remember to flip the cutlets halfway through to ensure even cooking. Heat the oil to 160°C (320°F). Add the cutlets one at a time and fry for 4 minutes until golden and cooked through. When ready, transfer to the cooling rack. Any excess oil will drip down.

Toss the cabbage in a bowl with the Worcestershire sauce, olive oil and seasoning.

Divide the pork cutlets between two individual plates without slicing. Pour the warm brown sauce generously over the top. Serve with shredded cabbage salad.

Soy Sauce Beef with Jammy Egg

My mother's *jangjorim* was deliciously salty with a sweet sauce that made you want to scoop it right onto the hot steaming bowl of rice. The pale golden margarine melted slowly on top of the rice, binding everything together into a shiny beige mush. The whites of the hard-boiled eggs she had thrown in turned a deep woody brown. Their pearly white skin was almost bouncy, with a slight chew from the glazing, and tasted as good as the shredded meat, if not better. But it also came with the brutally sacrificed yolk that had the interesting-looking moss green ring around it from overcooking.

I remember everything smelling strangely nutty and feeling slippery on the tongue. It ate smoothly, with the occasional salty bite of tender beef pleasantly cutting through the fat. And it was all a real treat.

Lean cuts of beef or pork are best for this dish as it is supposedly served at room temperature. Beef is first boiled with aromatics until tender, then torn into chunky strips before being braised in salty-sweet liquid seasoned with soy sauce and sugar.

Traditionally, the dish was made rather salty to ensure longer preservation of meat and was enjoyed in small quantities, like a condiment rather than a stew. It used to be said that properly made *jangjorim* would easily last for several weeks, though the eggs are best eaten sooner rather than later.

Rather than hard-boiling, I like to marinate the soft-boiled egg here for the jammy yolk. Both meat and eggs continue to marinate in the sauce and the flavour improves by the day.

Don't be tempted to braise the meat with the soy sauce right from the beginning, as the salty soy sauce will draw out the moisture from the meat if added too early, and make the meat tougher. As the dish cools down, the hardened fat can be skimmed off to yield a purer sauce.

Serves 6

600g (1lb 5oz) beef brisket or bavette
100g (3½oz) leek, cut in half crossways
100g (3½oz) daikon radish, cut into chunks
½ onion, skin on
5 garlic cloves, left whole
2 tsp roughly sliced ginger root
one 5 × 7.5cm (2 x 3in) piece of *dasima* (dried kelp)
1 tsp black peppercorns
1 litre (34fl oz/4 cups) water

For the sauce

3 tbsp golden granulated sugar
4 tbsp soy sauce
2 tbsp mirin
2 tsp English mustard
2 dried red chillies

For the eggs

1 tsp fine sea salt
1 tsp cider vinegar
6 eggs

To finish

sprinkling of toasted white sesame seeds

Pat the beef dry with kitchen paper to remove any sitting blood. Cut the beef into chunky pieces measuring about 5cm (¾in) square, ensuring the grain runs evenly lengthways. Place the beef, leek, daikon radish, onion, garlic, ginger, *dasima* and black peppercorns into a large saucepan. Fill with the water and bring to the boil. You will notice some scum rising to the surface as it reaches boiling point. Skim off the scum but don't worry too much – it will all sort itself out as it simmers. Lower the heat immediately and maintain a low simmer with small bubbles rising intermittently. Cook for 1½ hours with the lid ajar, or until tender. Remove the meat and set aside to cool.

Meanwhile, bring a pan of water to the boil for the eggs. Add the salt and vinegar to the pan, and carefully drop in the eggs. Stir briefly and cook for 6 minutes to yield soft-boiled eggs. Once done, drain. Roll or tap the eggs gently against the surface to crack the shells a little. Submerge the eggs in cold water to chill completely. When cooled down enough to handle, peel and set aside.

Carefully pass the meat cooking liquid through the fine sieve, reserving 600ml (20fl oz/2½ cups) of stock. Discard the aromatics. Save any extra stock for another time to use in soups and stews.

$\rightarrow$

STEAMED + BRAISED

When the meat has cooled down enough to handle, shred the pieces lengthways into fairly chunky pieces using two forks or your fingers. Set aside.

Pour the reserved stock into a saucepan. Add the sugar, soy sauce, mirin, mustard and dried red chillies. Whisk to combine. Add the meat and bring to the boil. Reduce the heat and simmer for 40 minutes over a low–medium heat. Stir occasionally. The sauce should have reduced significantly. Carefully stir in the eggs to warm briefly. Remove from the heat and leave it to cool before transferring to an airtight container. Ensure the mixture cools down completely before storing in the fridge; it will keep well for a good five days.

Though the dish is traditionally served cold or at room temperature, I like to serve it warm: just decant the desired amount and reheat gently but thoroughly, if you wish. Scatter with a pinch of toasted white sesame seeds before serving and eat with a bowl of plain steamed rice.

Gyeran Jjim

Steamed Egg

My mother used to steam her *gyeran jjim* in the steaming rice pot. A clingfilm-wrapped old china pot filled with loosened eggy mixture sat comfortably nestled amongst the perfectly washed pearly white grains of rice, with water carefully lapping round the bowl just a few centimetres above the base of cracked china. I suppose she figured that it was the simplest way to cook two things at the same time while she got on with stirring up a few other things on the hob.

Her *gyeran jjim* was usually seasoned with salted shrimps and had a deep umami taste of the ocean. She whisked in finely shredded young courgettes (zucchini) in summer, with burnished red speckles of *gochugaru* softly bleeding into the over-steamed egg. I would scoop out a big wobbly spoonful from the edges where the chilli flakes hadn't quite managed to invade and mush it into the perfectly plumped grains of rice. Soft porridge-like eggy rice was soothing and slipped down the throat like velvety custard. My mother's cooking was never fancy but always made us feel well fed with love. And I still find steamed egg as beautifully tender to the soul as it is to the mouth.

Although I admire my mother's crafty way of steaming her egg with rice, I quite like mine just barely set and creamy. Strain the loosened egg mixture through a fine sieve to help maintain the silkiness. I also prefer mine simply topped with finely sliced spring onions and some ginger for the fresh kick, but a handful of mushrooms is also great. The dish makes an excellent breakfast.

Makes 2 × 200ml (7fl oz) bowls

3 eggs
1 tbsp mirin
½ tsp golden granulated sugar
½ tsp sea salt flakes
½ tsp fish sauce
240ml (8fl oz/1 cup) Quick Stock (page 219) or *Dasima* & Mushroom Stock (page 220) or water

To finish
1 spring onion (scallion), green parts only, thinly sliced
a few thin julienne matchsticks of ginger root
a few drops of toasted sesame oil

Crack the eggs into a mixing bowl and lightly whisk without creating too many air bubbles.

Add the mirin, sugar, salt, fish sauce and stock. Whisk gently to combine, ensuring the sugar and salt are fully dissolved. Pass the egg mixture through a fine sieve into a jug with a pouring spout.

Carefully pour the egg mixture into two individual heatproof bowls: this gives me an opportunity to save one to steam another time, if I only need one portion, but feel free to use one large dish if you prefer.

Set your steamer. I use the flat steaming trivet inserted at the centre of my wok and my bowls sit on top. I fill the wok with just-boiled water, barely skimming the surface of the trivet so there is no direct contact between the water and the bowls, then cover the top with a lid to keep in the steam. Simmer for 7 minutes over a low heat to set the eggs with a nice wobble. If you are using one large bowl, you may want to cook for a few minutes longer.

Once the eggs are set to your liking, carefully lift the bowls out onto the heatproof surface. Top with some sliced spring onion and ginger, then finish with a few drops of toasted sesame oil just before serving.

Roasted Aubergine Salad

Gaji Namul

More traditionally, aubergines (eggplants) in this dish are steamed, cut in half lengthways (or quartered if large), until the flesh is completely soft. Once cooled down enough to handle, the steamed aubergines are usually torn by hand to create uneven surfaces that reveal different layers of the flesh, which in turn helps the flesh to absorb the dressing better. This particular texture of unevenness is considered to be what makes this dish great amongst keen cooks. I saw my mother skilfully tear the mounds of almost too-hot-to-touch aubergines without bother, before tossing them in the delicately fragrant dressing. This mouthwatering *banchan* often took centre stage in hot and humid late summer's evening meals and rejuvenated somewhat lacklustre appetites with its refreshing lightness.

The above technique is very much possible when you are working with Asian aubergines that boast thin skins and firmer flesh, but most Western varieties have much thicker and tougher skin, and the squishy flesh often turns into soggy mush when steamed till the skin feels tender enough. Even then, I find the skin quite tough and chewy. To rectify this, I have opted for abandoning the skin by roasting them in the oven to steam inside their own skins until the flesh of the aubergines is completely soft. Once done, the beautifully tender flesh is simply scooped out with ease.

Preheat a fan oven to 180°C (350°F/ gas 6).

Pierce the aubergine with a fork to make a few holes to prevent it from exploding. Place it in a baking tray and roast it for about 40 minutes, or until completely soft.

Meanwhile, combine all the ingredients for the dressing in a mixing bowl and set aside. I like to use a large bowl so I can directly scoop in the softened flesh of the cooked aubergine.

When the aubergine is done, it will look quite wrinkly on the outside and feel very floppy. Let it cool down a little so it's not fiercely hot to handle. Carefully peel off and discard the skin. Shred or mush the soft flesh with a fork, then stir it into the dressing to combine. Let it sit for a few minutes before serving to give it a chance to soak up some flavour.

It is excellent cold and keeps well for a couple of days in the fridge, stored in an airtight container.

Serves 2

1 large aubergine
 (eggplant)

For the dressing
2 tbsp soup or light
 soy sauce
1 tbsp toasted sesame oil
2 tsp golden granulated
 sugar
2 tsp rice wine vinegar
1 tsp toasted white
 sesame seeds
2 garlic cloves, minced
1 spring onion (scallion),
 thinly sliced

Soy Butter-Glazed Baby Potatoes

The delicious smell of buttery golden potatoes slowly caramelizing on a hot plate used to be the sure sign that we were on the road. Potatoes small enough to pick out with a toothpick; it was really nothing much more than a simple concoction of butter, salt and maybe a pinch of sugar (yes, really, sugar), but it was all the more enjoyable al fresco.

Sometimes, I think what we taste isn't just the flavours of the food itself. It is the seasons of wild flowers and rainfall around us; how the scorching sun or gentle breeze felt on our skins at the time; it's the living and breathing sound of life all around us and the warmth of people who make us feel happy. When I think of the taste of any dish, I think of the smells in the air and empty chatters queuing up for toilets, and the ice-cream on the tip of the nose of a merry child. I think memories of taste are about the small details of everything in between: vivid and dreamy all in one breath and, for that reason, so often hard to replicate.

This is my nostalgic plate of deliciousness, embellished with many a sunburnt beach holiday or carefree trip of youth. It sits somewhere between the butter-grilled potatoes that are a typical motorway service station snack sold across Korea and a soy-braised potato *banchan* dish, which I used to enjoy as a child. The sauce comes together quickly, so make it when the potato is ready, and serve with mounds of parmesan to contrast the sprinkle of sugar.

Serves 3–4

1 tbsp extra virgin olive oil
500g (1lb 2oz) baby
    potatoes
sea salt flakes, to season

For the sauce
3 tbsp water
1 tbsp soy sauce
20g (¾oz) unsalted butter
¼ tsp golden granulated
    sugar

To finish
liberal amount of finely
    grated parmesan
sea salt flakes, to season
snipped chives,
    to garnish

Preheat a fan oven to 180°C (350°F/gas 6).

Place the olive oil in a rimmed baking dish large enough to accommodate the potatoes snugly with little spaces in between. Put the cold baking dish of oil on the middle shelf in the oven for 10 minutes to heat up.

Put the potatoes in a large, lidded saucepan, Fill it with cold water to come 2cm (¾in) above the potatoes. Add a good pinch of salt and bring to the boil, then turn down the heat and simmer gently for about 8 minutes, or until the flesh of the potatoes has softened slightly. You don't want to cook the potatoes completely. Drain and set aside.

Carefully remove the hot baking dish from the oven and add the parboiled potatoes.

Give it a good stir to coat the potatoes evenly with the hot oil. Roast them for 35 minutes, or until tender.

To make the sauce, combine the water and soy sauce in a sauté pan. Let it come to bubble over a low heat. You should notice the small bubbles gather around the side. Slowly melt in the butter to emulsify. The sauce will have the colour of butterscotch. Toss in the roasted potatoes to glaze for a minute or two. Remove from the heat and stir in the sugar.

Transfer to a serving platter. Scatter generously with finely grated parmesan, a sprinkling of flaked sea salt and snipped chives. Serve warm as a snack or part of a spread for grilled skewers such as Chicken Skewers with Sesame Chicken Skin Crumbs (page 132) or *Doenjang* Lamb Skewers (page 128).

Dubu Jorim

Braised Tofu

My maternal grandmother was particularly good with tofu studded with sweetly seasoned minced pork. It was fried until the perfect shade of light golden brown, then slowly braised, doused in an oniony soy sauce until the slabs of tofu softly swelled, with no sign of the braising liquid left in the pan. She was a dainty cook that stuffed the tiny meatballs in the most rustic fashion, but was always utterly precise in her execution. Her old, wrinkly hands knew exactly how much things weighed and her fingertips co-ordinated gracefully in harmony with her eyes. I loved watching her cook, and especially watching her hands.

I remember my mother's tofu. It was unfussy and had more fiery bite to it from heaps of *gochugaru*; it was saucier than her mother's. She pan-fried large, well-salted slabs of tofu and braised them in fiercely bubbling liquid, with her soft pale hands tilting and scooping the sauce over the tofu every so often to keep it moist. Her tofu was juicy, always best eaten straight out of the pan. The hot steaming liquid dripped down my chin with the first bite and it was almost impossible to keep it in my mouth without blowing frantically to cool it down. It didn't matter anyway. I like my food steaming hot.

My *dubu jorim* probably does not taste anything like my grandmother's or my mother's. My memories are vivid but the flavours are faint, making it hard to replicate. But, as with the traditions of Korean home cooking, I hope there is an element of all of us weaved through to interconnect the three generations of mothers and daughters to the fourth, and so on.

Serves 2–4

396g (14oz) block
  of firm tofu
fine sea salt flakes,
  to season
1 tbsp vegetable oil
200ml (7fl oz/scant 1 cup)
  Quick Stock (page 219),
  Dasima & Mushroom
  Stock (page 220)
  or water

For the sauce
2 tbsp soy sauce
1 tbsp mirin
1 tsp *gochugaru* (Korean
  red pepper flakes)
1 tsp golden granulated
  sugar
1 tsp toasted sesame oil
½ tsp toasted white
  sesame seeds
¼ tsp freshly cracked
  black pepper
2 garlic cloves, minced

Pat dry the tofu with kitchen paper and slice the block in half lengthways, then slice evenly into about 2cm (¾in) thick slices. Lay the tofu slices on a tray lined with a sheet of kitchen paper, so it can soak up the excess moisture. Salt them generously, then leave to stand for 10 minutes.

Combine all the ingredients for the sauce in a bowl. Set aside.

Pat the salted tofu slabs dry with kitchen paper.

Heat the vegetable oil in a non-stick frying pan (skillet) large enough to accommodate the tofu in one single layer. Carefully lay the tofu slabs in the pan and fry for 5 minutes over a medium heat until golden on both sides, flipping halfway through.

Spoon the sauce over the fried tofu and carefully pour the stock or water into the edge of the pan. Simmer gently for 10–15 minutes over a low heat to allow the tofu to soften and absorb the flavour of the braising liquid. You may want to check from time to time to make sure the sauce is not reducing too quickly – add a touch more stock or water if so. Spoon the braising liquid over the tofu occasionally to keep it moist. It should appear plump with a little bit of sauce left in the pan. Remove from the heat.

Serve while warm with plain steamed rice, though it is perfectly good eaten cold, too. Leftovers can be stored in the fridge for a couple of days in an airtight container.

STEAMED + BRAISED

Ferments + Pickles

two

preserving season: a taste of home

I always dreamt about coming to England after reading *Wuthering Heights* under the duvet as a child. I imagined the wild and stormy green hills, and romanticized the views of ever-changing skies cast with black and grey clouds. In this faraway place across the ocean that I now call my home, people drank black tea with milk stirred through in shades of butterscotch biscuits. I learnt roasted chicken was for Sundays with gravy on the side and, in British pubs, you could order pints of beer without food, and that no one ever says 'how do you do?'. Yes, I really did say that once in a local pub in New Malden, just outside London. Timidly reaching my hand out to the lady behind the bar after painstakingly practising it under my breath for the tenth time. My cheeks flushed with embarrassment but there was also a certain kind of fire rising from the belly, too. I wanted to be better.

I didn't care if the taste of my mother's kimchi was fading slowly into the background. I didn't need to know where I came from, as long as I blended into these roads with red double-decker buses and low brick-built houses with manicured gardens in the suburbs. In these streets, every corner seemed wondrous – like the movies – and people spoke like the songs from the radio I had been reciting phonetically and with a great enthusiasm. All I wanted was to speak like everyone else, to truly live my dream, and to feel like one of them; us; whatever you want to call it.

For a long time, I did not cook rice at home. I ate bread and butter for the convenience instead of rice and kimchi, and keenly attempted to live the English life that I hoped would lead to my being accepted. Soon, the bank of words that I kept inside faded from my tongue. Each word swallowed wilfully, then regurgitated with a different sound into the language that I desperately wanted to vocalize.

I was certain that I would feel the sense of achievement when I no longer struggled. Instead, I felt lost, aching from the hollowed-out heart, not knowing who exactly I was supposed to be, parted and tangled in a mess of identity crisis. I thought I would be proud of this moment. But I craved the taste of my mother tongue in shame, unable to eloquently translate my feelings in Korean with vocabularies and sentences that were stuck back at the naïve age of nineteen.

I existed in a perpetual hunger that I could not feed properly. I bought and ate packets of instant noodles three days in a row and binged on a large pouch of kimchi straight out of the packet, staring into the distance with feelings I couldn't articulate or quantify, except that it was too salty, so I would end up drinking water in the same volume that I probably needed to cry out. And when I got fed up with the taste that did not deliver the home I desperately missed, I decanted the leftover kimchi into a plastic pot and returned, unsatisfied, to reluctantly chew on the bread slathered in thick, salty butter, wondering where I might find my mother tongue again.

I wrapped the plastic pot tightly with clingfilm to stop the pungent smell leaking and snuck it deep into the corner of the fridge where I would forget it for a while – until the next wave of cravings hit me hard and fast like a monthly period that I had no control over. Then, one day, I decided to make that old-forgotten kimchi into my mother's *kimchi jjigae* that was flavoured with anchovies, because even I knew soured kimchi was no good for anything else.

Tasteless salty cabbages, now perfectly soured, there was a certain kind of pungency that was particularly delicious when simmered gently, unveiling the time when it had evolved in depth of flavour: a characterful robustness that stands the test of time. Its fiery nature mellows but an assertive tanginess that is unique to each home comes

forward to show off the taste of the cook's hands that we call *sonmat*.

I ate that kimchi stew for a few days in a row, grieving in silence for what I had lost but also elated that I might finally have been reunited with the memories of taste that I instinctively knew belonged to my mother's kitchen. My mother's voice whispered softly in my head as I stirred; I saw the traces of my father loudly slurping the salty and tangy broth the usual way, sitting crossed-legged at the low dining table we used to sit around together.

I knew then that I would untangle the mess of my long-forgotten past, like a ghost looking for the home where it once belonged. I would find my own seasons to pickle garlic scapes and cucumbers; I would make my own small batch of kimchi to last the whole winter; and I would eventually find my own taste of home that I could imprint onto the muscles in my fingertips, so it would continue to live and breathe through a child of my own.

-

My mother fermented and pickled every season as they came and went, relying on (and trusting) changing temperature to speed up or slow down the process to influence the flavour. I remember her salting early cucumbers in spring in steaming hot brine and keeping them in the dark corner of her kitchen, while the radishes were preserved outside in the autumn. Her pickled cucumbers were sharply salty with a

strong briny smell that was deliciously piquant once it was rinsed and dressed in spicy *gochugaru* dressing. She made her kimchi with freshly shucked oysters and salted shrimps in winter; it fermented slowly under the earth to last until the following spring.

I would have liked to open this chapter of ferments and pickles by saying that this is one of those collections of precious family recipes that are handed down through the generations. But in truth, my journey of properly batching homemade kimchi and old-school pickles actually only began about seven years ago when I was struggling with my identity crisis after the birth of my daughter. I needed this catalyst to reconnect to my Korean roots and to explore and evaluate how I was going to raise a child of dual heritage to become truly dual – and food felt like the most tangible thing that I could count on.

The recipes here are the collections of my childhood memories and observations, which I have carefully attempted to translate into the tastes that I recognize as my home. In Korea, people believe kimchi tastes uniquely different in every home: kimchi is the taste of home.

Notes on Salting, Rinsing + Draining

Salting primarily removes the moisture from vegetables. As it loses water, the internal structure softens, especially for Chinese cabbage, allowing the kimchi paste to penetrate deeper into the flesh. Any unwanted bacteria will also be killed during salting, enabling longer preservation.

Rinsing after salting is important as it provides an opportunity to control the salinity and cleanliness; it removes any excess salt the cabbage may have absorbed.

Draining is often overlooked. People tend to treat this part of the process lightly or disregard it completely, but it is the final step that allows the vegetables to let out unwanted water to ensure the final concentration and texture of the kimchi. Let it sit in a wide colander to drain naturally and give it time to drain fully and thoroughly, without squeezing; any pressure applied will damage the structure of the cabbage thus resulting in improperly textured kimchi that is unpleasantly soft and mushy.

They are simple enough steps but require time and patience.

Notes on Kimchi Paste

There are many opinions on whether the use of flour paste or sugar is necessary. The main purpose of flour paste is to feed the good bacteria to develop more layers of flavour, rich in umami. It also helps to control the overall density of the final product. The small amount of sugar used in kimchi is to balance the flavour; the sugar is consumed by the good bacteria, then broken down during the fermentation process.

Kimchi paste can benefit from being made in advance so that the raw ingredients can mingle together to deepen the flavour. The unpleasant smell of rawness Koreans often associate with *gochugaru* – which loosely translates as grassiness (in a negative way) – mellows as it sits in the fridge, and the crimson red *gochugaru* swells to soften its raw edges and become more rounded.

I like to pound the garlic, ginger and chilli in a mortar and pestle to release their oil, using a pinch of salt as an abrasive to help me break down the flesh of the aromatics. It is the way my mother made her kimchi and there's a certain emotional attachment to the process that I want to preserve. For the convenience of the recipes, though, I have assumed you are using a food processor.

The seasoning of kimchi changes vastly from region to region. Whilst Seoul-style kimchi tends not to be either fiery or salty, more southern or coastal towns may use more salted fish products in the paste, yielding a more robust depth of flavour. Saltiness can dilute a great deal as it ferments, so taste the kimchi before storing it away – I prefer it a touch salty on the day rather than perfect.

Cut Cabbage Kimchi

When I first came to London over two decades ago, kimchi was not as readily available as it is now. I am proud and amazed to see the jars appearing in the local supermarkets and for it to have become an ingredient that most of us are familiar with. We've all learned how to weave the bold and funky flavours of kimchi into the Western pantry and there is definitely a healthy appetite and steady growth for making our own at home, which is just so wonderful to witness.

The most classic type of kimchi we mainly associate with is made with Chinese cabbage, which is either quartered with its leaves attached to the core and swaddled tightly like a baby before being packed in the jar (*pogi kimchi*), or simply cut into bite-size pieces for convenience. Generally speaking, the fermentation process takes a little longer for the former to reach the optimum population of lactic acid bacteria, making it suitable to keep large batches for a longer period of time. Meanwhile, the bacterial growth happens more quickly in cut cabbages and therefore the flavours develop more quickly, which is really effective for smaller batches.

As home refrigerator temperatures constantly fluctuate with daily use, the inconsistent temperature can lead to poor flavour in large batches. I therefore prefer to make a small batch of cut kimchi more frequently. Plus, there is no need for a red-stained chopping board or messy fingers with cut kimchi!

The process does take up a whole day but is straightforward and mostly hands-off. Please do not rush salting, rinsing and draining – I really think these first three steps do determine the end result, so please give it the love and respect it deserves.

Makes enough to fill a 2.5–3 litre (85–100fl oz/ 10½–12½ cup) container

For the salting
1.5kg (3lb 2oz) Chinese cabbage
130g (4½oz) coarse sea salt
2 litres (70fl oz/8 cups) water

For the flour paste
180ml (6fl oz/¾ cup) Quick Stock (page 219)
1½ tbsp glutinous rice flour

For the kimchi paste
35g (1¼oz) garlic cloves, crushed
30g (1oz) ginger root, roughly chopped
1 long red chilli, about 20g (¾oz), roughly chopped
2 tbsp fish sauce (or soy sauce to make it vegan)
50g (1¾oz) gochugaru (Korean red pepper flakes)
30g (1oz/2 tbsp) Demerara sugar
1 tsp shrimp paste (substitute with barley miso to make vegan)

For the kimchi
400g (14oz) daikon radish, julienned
100g (3½oz) carrot, julienned
½ onion, thinly sliced
4 spring onions (scallions), chopped

To prepare the cabbage, remove any wilted green outer leaves. Slice the base of the cabbage in half lengthways and gently pull them apart to tear away the leaves to split naturally. The edges will look gnarly and uneven – that is exactly what we want. Then halve it again exactly the same way, so you end up with a quartered cabbage. Remove the cores and cut into fairly large bite-size pieces; especially the softer ends. Transfer the cut cabbages to a large mixing bowl or container, layering with the salt as you go along. Use up all the salt. Pour the water over the cabbage and press it down gently to submerge. Cover and leave it to soak in the brine for 4 hours, turning it over halfway through to ensure even salting.

Meanwhile, place the stock and glutinous rice flour in a small saucepan and whisk until smooth. Bring to a gentle simmer over a low heat, stirring constantly to make sure the flour doesn't clump together. After a couple of minutes, you will feel the heaviness of liquid starting to cling. Continue to cook and stir the paste for 5 minutes or so until it thickens to the consistency of runny custard and the colour begins to turn a little more translucent than opaque white. Remove from the heat and set aside to cool completely.

To make the kimchi paste, blitz together the garlic, ginger, red chilli and fish sauce (or soy sauce) in a food processor until smooth.

→

Ferments + Pickles

Transfer to a lidded container and stir in the *gochugaru*, sugar and shrimp paste (or barley miso), along with the cooled flour paste. Combine well and refrigerate until needed.

After 4 hours, add the julienned radish and carrot to the cabbage, and submerge completely in the brine. Leave to soak for a further 30 minutes.

By now, the cabbages should have softened enough that you can bend them easily without snapping them. Drain everything, rinse with fresh water, then drain again. Repeat the process two more times so that you have thoroughly cleaned the cabbages, radishes and carrots. Let the vegetables naturally drain the water out fully – this may take up to an hour. Never squeeze the water out by hand as it will damage the structure of the cabbage, resulting an improperly textured kimchi.

Once fully drained, transfer to a large mixing bowl or container. Add the onion and kimchi paste. Wear gloves to toss everything together by hand to incorporate the paste into the vegetables, gently massaging them to coat evenly. Once well combined, stir in the spring onions.

Transfer the kimchi into a clean jar or two – it doesn't need to be sterilized but should be thoroughly clean and bone dry. Tightly pack but don't fill completely up to the brim.

Swirl about 100ml (3½fl oz/scant ½ cup) of water into the empty mixing bowl if there's a bit of paste left, scrape to rinse and pour over the kimchi. Gently press the top to ensure the kimchi is submerged in juice.

Kimchi will start the fermentation process as it sits in the jar. Let it sit at room temperature, away from the direct sun, for two days if the weather is cool or one day if warm, then transfer to store in the fridge to slowly ferment for about ten days. Kimchi will continue to develop the flavours as it matures, and the character changes dramatically as it ages. The preference for how ripe or young you like your kimchi differs from person to person. I like mine at about three weeks into the fermentation, when the gentle but pronounced tanginess kicks in, but you might prefer it more fresh or even more aged. So please do taste at different stages to see at which stage you like it best.

Kimchi will keep well for up to three months in a fridge set at 4°C (39°F) without compromising the quality too much, providing you have taken utmost care to decant it with clean utensils each time and have left the rest of the batch refrigerated at a constant temperature.

Cubed Daikon Radish Kimchi

Kkakdugi

It is said the name *kkakdugi* was given to this dish because of the way radish is diced into cubes. I adore the way it sounds when you say it out loud. To me, the sound has sharp edges that give out the sense of evenness which feels completely right to describe the dish.

In Korea, autumn is considered the best season for radish as they are naturally sweeter and crunchier than summer varieties, making it perfect for a quick batch of radish kimchi to tide over the gaps while people await the arrival of winter cabbages for the *gimjang* season.

When radishes undergo a slow fermentation process, their perfectly squared corners soften a little; the spiciness of radish also mellows, pushing its sweet character forward to take the lead. Over time, fresh flavours evolve to build a robust savouriness and the kimchi develops a refreshing, almost effervescent tanginess that pairs particularly well with rich, milky-white bone broths such as oxtail soup. Well-matured *kkakdugi* also makes great kimchi fried rice.

You can use any seasonal varieties available if daikon is not around. Tokyo turnips are especially delicious with their slightly bitter leaves thrown in, or kohlrabi can also be made more or less the same way. Just remember to adjust the salting time to ensure they are not over- or under-brined.

Peel, top and tail the radishes. Slice into 2cm (¾in) thick discs, then dice each disc into about 2cm (¾in) cubes. Transfer to a large mixing bowl or container and massage the salt and sugar in to coat evenly. Pour the water over the cubed radishes and press down gently to submerge. Cover and leave to soak for 1 hour, turning it halfway through to ensure even salting.

Meanwhile, place the stock and glutinous rice flour in a small saucepan and whisk until smooth. Bring to a gentle simmer over a low heat, stirring constantly to make sure the flour doesn't clump together. After a couple of minutes, you will feel the heaviness of the liquid starting to cling. Continue to cook and stir the paste for 5 minutes or so until it thickens to the consistency of runny custard and the colour begins to turn a little more translucent than opaque white. Remove from the heat and set aside to cool completely.

To make the kimchi paste, blitz together the garlic, ginger, red chilli and soy sauce in a food processor until smooth. Transfer to a lidded container and stir in the *gochugaru*, sugar and barley miso, along with the cooled flour paste. Combine well and refrigerate for 1 hour or until needed.

Carefully drain the salty brine away from the radishes without rinsing, then transfer them to a large mixing bowl. Add the kimchi paste and wear gloves to work the radishes by hand to massage in the paste so that the crimson red *gochugaru* can penetrate into the flesh of the white, cubed radishes. Once combined well, check for seasoning and adjust it with fine salt. You should be able to notice the saltiness, as radishes will release more water during the fermentation process; I found about 1 teaspoon is enough.

$\rightarrow$

Makes enough to fill a 1.5 litre (50fl oz/ 6 cup) container

For the salting
1–1.2kg (2lb 4oz–2lb 6oz) daikon radish
2 tbsp coarse sea salt
2 tbsp golden granulated sugar
500ml (17fl oz/2 cups) water

For the flour paste
180ml (6fl oz/¾ cup) Quick Stock (page 219)
1½ tbsp glutinous rice flour

For the kimchi paste
35g (1¼oz) garlic cloves, crushed
30g (1oz) ginger root, roughly chopped
1 long red chilli, about 20g (¾oz), roughly chopped
2 tbsp soy sauce
50g (1¾oz) *gochugaru* (Korean red pepper flakes), or to taste
30g (1oz) Demerara sugar
1 tsp barley miso

To finish
1 tsp fine sea salt
4 spring onions (scallions), chopped
100ml (3½fl oz/scant ½ cup) water

When you are happy with the seasoning, add the spring onions and toss everything together.

Transfer the kimchi into a large, clean jar (or two smaller ones) – it doesn't need to be sterilized but should be thoroughly clean and bone dry. Tightly pack but don't fill right up to the brim. Swirl the remaining water into the empty mixing bowl where you have a bit of paste left. Scrape to rinse, then pour over the kimchi. Gently press the top to ensure any air pockets between the cubed radishes are removed and that the ingredients are submerged in juice.

Radish kimchi can be eaten almost immediately, but I think the flavour improves so much more over time that it is worth waiting until it matures. It will start the fermentation process as it sits in the jar.

Let it sit at room temperature, away from the direct sun, for three days if the weather is cool and one or two days if warm, to kick start the fermentation process. In due course, you should notice lively air bubbles forming in the jars, which usually is a good sign. Transfer to store in the fridge to slowly ferment for about two weeks, checking occasionally to taste, to see at which stage you like it best.

It will keep well for up to three months in the fridge set at 4°C (39°F), providing you have taken utmost care to decant it with clean utensils each time and left the rest of the batch refrigerated at a constant temperature.

White Kimchi

My father occasionally used to take us to a lovely barbecue place called Nak Won Garden near Kimpo Airport, where I first tasted white kimchi. You drive through the gated entrance in the middle of the hustle and bustle of city life that magically turns into beautifully manicured fields of greens and trees. Soon you discover another door leading into the traditional-looking houses with curved slate roofs and decoratively framed windows. It is the kind of place where you take important guests for a special meal; whether that be a table-side barbecue under the posh wooden gazebo or the full spread of a traditional dinner sitting in the private dining room.

White kimchi is delicately flavoured with a perfect balance of sweet and sour and an almost floral piquancy. It is distinctively fresh with a palate-cleansing quality. With its pale stems and lemon-yellow, frilly ends coiled so elegantly, to me white kimchi has always felt like understated sophistication, not least because I associate the dish with the upmarket restaurant.

Its fruity, sweet and sour taste pairs particularly well with soy-marinated grilled meat dishes such as LA Short Ribs (page 126) or Grilled Meat Patties (page 131). More traditional recipes tend to call for the addition of fish sauce and salted shrimps; I keep mine simply seasoned with salt, as I think slowly brewed *dasima* stock adds plenty of umami, but do feel free to experiment. The saltiness will dull down as it matures in the fridge, so make sure to season enough to taste the hint of salt.

Makes enough to fill a 2 litre (70fl oz/8 cup) container

For the salting
1kg (2lb 4oz) Chinese cabbage
130g (4oz) coarse sea salt
2 litres (70fl oz/8 cups) water

For the flour paste
180ml (6fl oz/¾ cup) Quick Stock (page 219)
1½ tbsp glutinous rice flour

For the kimchi juice
½ onion, roughly chopped
½ Asian pear, peeled, cored and roughly chopped
20g (¾oz) garlic cloves, crushed
15g (½oz) ginger root, roughly chopped
400ml (13fl oz/generous 1½ cups) Quick Stock (page 219), cooled
30g (1oz/2 tbsp) white granulated sugar
1 tbsp fine sea salt

For the kimchi filling
150g (5oz) daikon radish, julienned
4 spring onions (scallions), cut into 4cm (1½in) batons
2 long red chillies, deseeded and julienned

To prepare the cabbage, remove any wilted green outer leaves. Slice the base of the cabbage in half lengthways and gently pull apart to tear away the leaves to split. The edges will look gnarly and uneven – that is exactly what we want. Then halve it again in exactly the same way, so you end up with quartered cabbages. Trim the base a little, ensuring the leaves are still attached to the core. Transfer the cabbages to a large mixing bowl or container one by one, layering the salt in between the leaves near to the head as you go along. Use up all the salt. Pour the water over the cabbages and press down gently to submerge. Cover and leave in the brine for 5 hours, or up to 8 hours in cooler months, turning the cabbages over halfway through to ensure even salting.

Meanwhile, place the stock and glutinous rice flour in a small saucepan.

Whisk together until smooth and bring to a gentle simmer over a low heat, stirring constantly to make sure the flour doesn't clump together. After a couple of minutes, you will feel the heaviness of the liquid starting to cling. Continue to cook and stir the paste for 3–5 minutes or so until it thickens to the consistency of runny custard. When the colour of the mixture becomes more translucent than opaque white, remove it from the heat and set aside to cool completely.

To make the kimchi juice, blitz together the onion, pear, garlic and ginger in a food processor until smooth. Place the completely cooled stock in a large mixing bowl. Set a fine sieve over the bowl and lay a muslin or cheesecloth over the sieve. Carefully pour the puréed mixture into the cloth-lined sieve.

→

Secure the cloth tightly from the top so you can start wringing it to push out the liquid from the purée into the stock. Squeeze as hard you can to extract as much liquid as possible, pressing on the solids. Once all the liquid is collected, discard the pulp. Add the flour paste and stir to combine. Add the sugar, and the salt to taste. Refrigerate until needed.

After 5 hours, check if the cabbages have softened enough so that you can bend them easily without snapping them. If not, leave them to brine for longer until softened. When ready, drain everything and rinse with fresh water, then drain again. Repeat the process two more times so that you have thoroughly cleaned the cabbages. Lay the cabbages open-side down so the water can naturally drain out fully – this may take up to an hour or two. Never squeeze the water out by hand as it will damage the structure of the cabbage and result in an improperly textured kimchi.

Meanwhile, combine the ingredients for the kimchi filling in a wide, shallow, rimmed tray or bowl.

Once the kimchi is fully drained, layer a small amount of kimchi filling in between the leaves, then transfer to a large jar or container – it doesn't need to be sterilized but should be thoroughly clean and bone dry. Tightly pack but don't fill right up to the brim.

Pour the kimchi juice over the top. Gently press the top to ensure the kimchi is submerged in juice. Depending on the container you are using, the cabbages may float up. If so, place a heavy plate on top to weigh them down.

Kimchi will start the fermentation process as it sits in the jar. Let it sit at room temperature, away from the direct sun, for three days if the weather is cool and one day if it is warm, before transferring to the fridge to ferment for at least a couple more days. It will continue to develop the flavours as it matures and the character changes, so do make sure to taste at different stages to see which you prefer.

To serve, remove the cabbage from the jar and cut away the core. You can keep them as whole, individual leaves to wrap meat to eat, like *ssam* (page 124) or slice the cabbage into bite-size pieces to enjoy.

It will keep well for a couple of months in the fridge at 4°C (39°F) without compromising the quality too much, providing you have taken utmost care of decanting it with clean utensils each time and leaving the rest of the batch refrigerated at a constant temperature.

Water Kimchi

Chilled water kimchi tastes deeply cleansing with a delicate salinity and effervescence coming from the fermentation. I have known my father slurp bowlful after bowlful, highly praising its refreshing taste and subtle sweetness, which comes from the fruit and sugar. Back then, I didn't think much of it. I was only able to taste the muted salt and sour, which I then categorized as nothingness, unable to appreciate the beauty of its delicate nature.

The name *nabak* is an old word that describes the way vegetables are cut into thin squares. It is said that the dish was originally made only with radish as the main vegetable. The dish was more commonly enjoyed during spring, as in winter we would have served the saltier *dongchimi* (fermented water kimchi made only with radish). More typically, the water will carry a red-tinged hue from the *gochugaru* dissolved in water which passes through the cheesecloth. However, I prefer the cleaner taste that comes from fresh red chilli, while beetroot does the great job of delivering the exquisitely delightful magenta water that is so uplifting and sweet.

Do experiment with other vegetables – I use a total of 600g (1lb 5oz) of seasonal vegetables. Chinese cabbage or crunchier breakfast radishes are good alternatives; carrots also add lovely sweetness. Tangy apple will be a great addition, as well as bitter Italian turnip tops. Just remember to salt the vegetables and to add the fruits last without salting, and eat them fridge-cold and as soon as they are ready.

Prepare the vegetables. Peel, top and tail the beetroots, then cut them in half (or quarter if large) and slice them into 5mm (¼in) thick pieces. Peel, top and tail the radish, cut into 4cm (1½in) discs, then cut each disc into 2.5cm (1in) wide batons, then each baton into 5mm (¼in) dice. Transfer both to a large jar or container that you will keep the kimchi in – it doesn't need to be sterilized but should be thoroughly clean and bone dry. Massage with the salt to coat evenly. Cover and leave for 30 minutes.

To make the kimchi juice, blitz together the apple, red chilli, garlic and ginger in a food processor until smooth. Place the water in a large mixing bowl. Set a fine sieve over the bowl and lay a muslin or cheesecloth over the sieve. Pour the puréed mixture into the cloth-lined sieve. Secure the cloth tightly so you can start to push out the liquid from the purée into the water. Squeeze as hard you can to extract as much liquid as possible. Once all the liquid is collected, discard the pulp. Add the

sugar, and salt to taste, ensuring you season enough to taste the hint of salt.

After 30 minutes, the beetroots and radishes should have gone a little limp from salting. Scatter the red chilli and spring onion on top. Pour the kimchi juice over the top to submerge everything.

The kimchi will start the fermentation process in the jar. Let it sit at room temperature, away from direct sun, for three or four days if the weather is cool and two days if warm, before transferring to the fridge to continue fermenting for at least a couple more days. It will continue to develop the flavours as it matures and the character changes, so do make sure to taste at different stages to see what you like best. It will keep well for about six weeks in the fridge set at 4°C (39°F) without compromising the quality too much, providing you have taken care to decant it with clean utensils each time and leave the rest of the batch refrigerated at a constant temperature.

Makes enough to fill a 2 litre (70fl oz/8 cup) container

For the salting
250g (9oz) beetroots (beets)
350g (12oz) daikon radish
1 tbsp coarse sea salt

For the kimchi juice
½ eating (dessert) apple, peeled, cored and roughly chopped
20g (¾oz) mild red chilli, roughly chopped
2 garlic cloves, minced
1 tsp roughly chopped ginger root
1 litre (34fl oz/4 cups) water
1 tbsp white granulated sugar
1 tbsp fine sea salt

To finish
½ mild red chilli, deseeded and cut into thin strips
2 spring onions (scallions), cut into 5cm (2in) batons

White Cabbage + Apple Kimchi

The idea of cabbage and apple in kimchi format might sound a little strange to some, but if you can imagine the more common combination of tangy coleslaw made with fine shreds of crunchy cabbages and tart juicy apples, hopefully, you will find the dish a little easier to taste.

The texture of cabbage here is carefully manipulated twice: first by brief salting, followed by gentle massaging by hand to further coax the fibres to soften enough to soak up the flavours. It retains a refreshing bite that is livelier than sauerkraut, with the occasional hit of fruity apple layering the enjoyable fizzy sweetness – I could eat a jarful on its own like a salad. Whilst the flavours do continue to deepen and develop a refreshing tanginess as it matures, overall the taste remains mild even after a few weeks of fermentation. If you are new to kimchi, I think this will make a good introduction; it's also really easy to make with a handful of readily available ingredients.

Autumn is a particularly good time for a batch when in-season cabbages are naturally sweet and juicy, and the apples are plentiful. Don't be tempted to use too much fish sauce, as it will interfere with the fresh taste of apple. This is not the type of kimchi you will want to keep for long: enjoy it within six weeks.

Makes enough to fill a 1.5 litre (50fl oz/6 cup) container

For the salting
½ white cabbage, about 500g (1lb 4oz)
1½ tbsp coarse sea salt
500ml (17fl oz/2 cups) water

For the kimchi paste
25g (¾oz) garlic cloves, minced
2 tsp roughly sliced ginger root
2 tsp fish sauce
3 tbsp *gochugaru* (Korean red pepper flakes)
2 tsp Demerara sugar

For the kimchi
2 apples, skin left on (I like fuji, golden delicious or pink lady)
½ onion, thinly sliced
2 spring onions (scallions), chopped
100ml (3½fl oz/scant ½ cup) water

Prepare the cabbage by removing any wilted outer leaves. Slice the cabbage in half lengthways so you have two wedges. Remove the cores and dice them into bite-size pieces. Transfer the cut cabbages to a large mixing bowl. Dissolve the salt into the water, then pour over the cabbages and press down firmly to submerge. Cover and leave to brine for 1 hour, turning halfway through to ensure even salting.

To make the kimchi paste, blitz together the garlic, ginger and fish sauce in a food processor until smooth. Transfer to a lidded container and stir in the *gochugaru* and sugar. Combine well and refrigerate until needed.

Meanwhile, quarter the apples and remove the cores. Slice each quartered apple into fairly large chunks – if cut too small, they will become mushy during the fermentation process. Set aside.

After 1 hour, the cabbage should have softened. Carefully drain away the salty brine without rinsing, then transfer to a large mixing bowl. Add the kimchi paste and wear gloves to work the cabbages by hand, squeezing firmly to encourage the cabbages to soften as you massage in the paste. Cabbages do not tend to release a lot of water by themselves during fermentation; I found this process really helps to create a good texture and juicy kimchi. Once well combined, add the apples, onion and spring onions. Toss everything together to coat evenly.

Transfer the kimchi to a clean jar – it doesn't need to be sterilized but should be thoroughly clean and bone dry. Tightly pack but don't fill right to the brim. Swirl around the water in the empty mixing bowl where you have a bit of paste left. Scrape to rinse and pour over the kimchi. Gently press the top to ensure the kimchi is submerged.

Let it sit at room temperature, away from the direct sun, for one day, then transfer to store in the fridge to slowly ferment for about ten days. It is perfectly fine to eat immediately, albeit very fresh-tasting. The characters of cabbage and apple will change as it ages, developing a really good level of tanginess after two weeks.

Ferments + Pickles

Pickled Cucumber

Oiji

Traditionally, the sour taste of these pickled cucumbers comes from the saltwater-based fermentation: a long process that requires the vats of brine to be decanted at a certain point to be reboiled then poured again for the concentrated salinity that ensures a good texture and longer preservation. It yields a remarkably crunchy pickle, but is very salty so needs a soak in a freshwater bath to remove the saltiness prior to its final use. These pickled cucumbers are used as an ingredient to be made into different dishes or as a side pickle.

Over recent years, a convenient method of pickling without water has become more popular as it is much easier and more convenient. A simple concoction of vinegar-laced sugar and salt brine coaxes the cucumbers to lose their natural moisture so they shrink, the flesh shrivels and the skin becomes wrinkly. In as little as three days, the refreshing character of watery cucumbers is transformed into a completely different kind of crunchy, with a pleasingly chewy bite that is commonly described as *kkodeul kkodeul* in Korean.

I am not specifying the size of container you need for this as it depends on the size of the cucumbers you are using. It is not a crucial factor. Use a flat container rather than a jar, though, so you can lay the cucumbers flat to ensure even coverage.

Top and tail the cucumbers, if you wish, but keep them whole. Arrange the cucumbers nice and flat in a snug container or resealable bag.

Sprinkle the sugar and salt over the top, then pour in the vinegar and sake. Cover and leave to sit at room temperature, away from the direct sun, for three days, turning daily to ensure the cucumbers are evenly saturated in the brine.

Cucumbers will naturally release a fair amount of water as they pickle and shrink in size, looking more yellow than green. If you have started them in a resealable bag, after three days, transfer them to a suitable container, including all the liquid, and store it in the fridge. Once chilled completely, the pickles can be eaten, though I think the flavours develop nicely after a week. Discard the brine after ten days – the cucumbers will keep well for about a month.

Makes about 600g (1lb 5oz)

500g (1lb 2oz) Kirby cucumbers (short and bumpy cucumbers often sold as pickling cucumbers)
75g (2½oz/heaped ⅓ cup) golden granulated sugar
15g (½oz) coarse sea salt
75ml (2½fl oz/5 tbsp) cider vinegar
2 tbsp sake

Ferments + Pickles 87

Spicy Pickled Cucumber Salad

Oiji Muchim

I think the wrinkly flesh and skin of pickled cucumbers makes the most perfect canvas for the spicy seasoning to invade deeply into every nook and cranny of its uneven surface. The prominent flavours of salty and sour pair brilliantly with fruity *gochugaru* and savoury sesame oil, making it a mouthwatering accompaniment to rice.

Serves 4

300g (12oz) Pickled Cucumber (page 87), sliced into rounds
1 tbsp *gochugaru* (Korean red pepper flakes)
1 tsp golden granulated sugar
2 tsp toasted sesame oil
1 tsp toasted white sesame seeds
2 garlic cloves, minced
1 spring onion (scallion), thinly sliced

Place all the ingredients in a mixing bowl and toss together to combine by hand, massaging firmly to distribute the seasoning evenly. You can serve immediately or store in the fridge to enjoy later. It will keep well in the fridge for up to five days.

Pictured opposite.

Soy Sauce Pickled Onions

Yangpa Jangajji

You can use any kind of onions here. Once lightly pickled, the strong, acrid taste of onion softens; I found the dish particularly refreshing. It pairs well with most things, lending an almost palate-cleansing respite in between mouthfuls. An ancient old technique of preserving in hot brine plays a key role in retaining the snappy texture.

It might be worth noting that traditional practice is to reboil the soy sauce brine at around day 3 to re-concentrate the salinity, which is believed to encourage the longer preservation of vegetables. Reboiled brine should be completely cooled before being poured over the vegetables for the second time round. I skip this process most of the time when I know the pickles are to be consumed in a relatively short period of a month or two. Serve a generous amount of the pickling juice on the side for Mung Bean Pancake (page 42) to saturate each bite-sized piece in the tangy sauce to cut through the richness. They are wonderful together.

Makes enough to fill two 350ml (12¼fl oz/1½ cup) sterilized heatproof containers

320g (11oz) onion, sliced into bite-sized wedges
½ unwaxed lemon, thinly sliced
125ml (4fl oz/½ cup) water
125ml (4fl oz/½ cup) soy sauce
50g (1¾oz/¼ cup) golden granulated sugar
50ml cider vinegar

Place the sliced onions and lemons into a sterilized heatproof jar or container.

Place the water, soy sauce and sugar into a small saucepan. Whisk together to combine and bring to a gentle simmer over a low heat to dissolve the sugar. Once hot, stir in the vinegar. Remove from the heat and pour over the onions and lemons. Press down gently to submerge them in the brine. Put the lid on ajar and let it cool down a little before securing the top properly.

Let the pickle sit at room temperature, away from the direct sun, for one day, then transfer to store in the fridge. It will be ready to eat from about day three, though the flavours will deepen with time, so do taste it at different stages to gauge your preference.

Beetroot-Stained Pickled Radish

My maternal grandmother used to have an old-school Korean fried chicken shop in the local market that she ran with her friend. The menu was non-existent; just a simple no-frills takeaway affair of whole fried chicken served with a sachet of salt seasoning for dipping, and a large pouch of sweet pickled radish, which she religiously prepared from home. I suspect she did not want anyone to know the secrets of her saccharine-sweet, crunchy pickles, though she was always generous enough to explain to her curious-eyed first grandchild what she was looking for when she tasted her pickling juice. Her radishes were perfectly sharp with a good bite, matured in a well-balanced brine that sang the high notes of sweet and sour. It cut through the grease-licked crust of deep-fried chicken and made it taste brighter.

Just a few thin slices of beetroot are all you need to make radishes blush gorgeously with the cheerful hue of magenta pink. It's not enough to flavour the radish but just enough to make you smile.

The way in which you prepare the radish transforms the same recipe into multiple pickles. Slice the radish into mandoline-thin discs to create what we call a *ssam mu* for Korean barbecue, to use as a vessel to wrap the meat. Cut it into thin strips to use as a delicious garnish for both Buckwheat Noodles in Icy Pink Broth (page 184) and Spicy Cold Noodles (page 188).

Add the vinegar right at the end to avoid boiling, so that the bright acidity is not lost in the heat. Used pickling juice can be reboiled once with slightly adjusted seasoning to pickle other vegetables. It can also be repurposed into a dipping sauce, combined with a touch of soy sauce.

Makes enough to fill a 1 litre (34fl oz/4 cup) sterilized heatproof container

500g (1lb 2oz) daikon radish
5 thin slices of unwaxed lemon
3 thin slices of raw beetroot (beet)
200ml (7fl oz/scant 1 cup) water
100g (3½oz/½ cup) white granulated sugar
1 tsp sea salt flakes
100ml (3½fl oz/scant ½ cup) cider vinegar

Peel, top and tail the radish, then slice into 2cm (¾in) thick discs, then cut each disc into 2cm (¾in) dice. Transfer the radishes into a sterilized heatproof jar or container, tucking slices of lemon and beetroot in between the radishes.

Put the water, sugar and salt into a small saucepan. Whisk together to combine and bring to a gentle simmer over a low heat until the sugar has fully dissolved – about 4 minutes. Once hot, stir in the vinegar, then warm up the liquid for a minute so the brine is hot but not boiling.

Remove from the heat and pour over the radishes, pressing down gently to submerge in the brine. Put the lid on ajar and let it cool down a little before securing the top properly.

Let the pickle sit at room temperature, away from the direct sun, for two days, then transfer to store in the fridge. Once chilled completely, the pickles are ready to eat. They will keep well in the fridge for two weeks.

Rhubarb Cho Jeorim

Anise Pickled Rhubarb

Brilliantly tart rhubarb laced with sweet orange and star anise here has an almost floral sweetness. The mouth-puckering sourness of rhubarb softens when pickled and becomes pleasantly zippy. It eats almost like an unripe plum – in a good way – with a satisfying crunch. I like to eat them with Grilled Salt-Cured Mackerel (page 152).

Makes enough to fill a 700ml (24fl oz/ scant 3 cup) sterilized heatproof container

400g (14oz) rhubarb
200ml (7fl oz/scant 1 cup) water
100g (3½oz/½ cup) white granulated sugar
1 tsp sea salt flakes
2 strips of fresh orange peel
2 star anise
100ml (3½fl oz/scant ½ cup) cider vinegar

To prepare the rhubarb, cut the stalks into 5cm (2in) long batons, then halve each one to cut it into thin strips. Transfer the stripped rhubarb into a sterilized heatproof jar or container.

Put the water, sugar and salt into a small saucepan. Whisk together to combine and add the orange peel and star anise. Bring to a gentle simmer over a low heat until the sugar has fully dissolved – about 4 minutes. Once hot, stir in the vinegar, then warm the liquid up for a minute so the brine is hot but not boiling.

Remove from the heat and pour over the rhubarb, pressing down gently to submerge in the brine. Put the lid on ajar and let it cool down a little before securing the top properly.

Let the pickle sit at room temperature, away from the direct sun, for one day, then transfer to store in the fridge. The pickles will be ready to eat after two days. They will keep well in the fridge for two weeks.

Ferments + Pickles

Soups + Stews

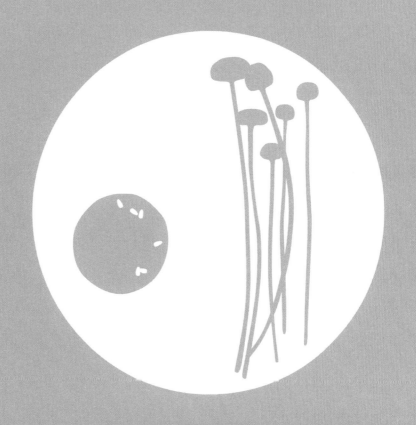

three

to scoop + slurp, while steaming hot

I'm sitting alone in my softly lit north-facing kitchen, accompanied by the reassuring sound of a gently simmering stockpot. The sky above me is cheerfully blue with noticeable chill in the air that is edging sharply into winter. It is November in London, after all. The hum of the bubbling pot sounds much like rainfall softly pattering onto the ground. A certain kind of smell pervades the kitchen as the stock steeps gently in the pan. Steaming window panes cocoon the kitchen; it feels cosy in here. I notice the small bubbles rise intermittently; a sure sign that tells me it is doing its thing at the right temperature. The only task asked of me is to occasionally skim the scum that rises and gathers around the edge of the pan – and to be patient.

I remember the house where we once lived, way back when I was around the age my daughter is now. The front door opened immediately into the small, old-fashioned kitchen with bare cemented walls and a tiny window that looked out onto the street. My mother's kitchen was dark and dimly lit, with only a little round bulb that flickered like a fluttering butterfly as you switched it on; like a dancing cue to the cook to perform where she would waltz through, turning and twisting her limbs around her pots and pans. Basked gloriously in the gentle beam of dusty winter sunshine, I saw my mother meticulously prepare the bones and honeycomb beef tripe in her less-than-well-equipped kitchen. It made our house smell of boiled bones for days on end, and we ate the lusciously milky

white bone broths on repeat until the very last bone was properly sucked out, to nourish us from inside out.

In that tiny kitchen with its less than practical coal-lit furnace and crappy old oil burner, my mother cooked rustic anchovy-flavoured kimchi *jjigae* (Kimchi Stew with Pork Belly – page 115). Her kimchi stew was briny and balanced with nose-tingling tanginess. We ate birthday soup (Seaweed Soup with Mussels – page 102) for breakfast on our birthdays and on other occasions worthy enough of beef, she fed us the most tender, soy-braised ribs. We frequently ate northern-style pulped soybean stew with overripe kimchi that was lusciously softened in rendered pork fat. It was subtly nutty and creamy, but with a distinctively grainy texture that I wasn't particularly keen on. That once food of poor has now become one the most fashionable dishes, one that everyone wants to slurp for good health.

My mother stirred up her own potion of crimson red *gochujang* paste before the arrival of warm spring days to stock up her pantry. Without fail, she reserved the last run of starchy water from her rice after rinsing to make her *doenjang jjigae* (Everyday *Doenjang* Stew – page 116). My mother's food had a charm of the good and proper countryside she grew up in, embellished generously with my father's northern soul and his upbringing in what was then the poorest part of Seoul. And I know it was in that house that I held a kitchen knife for the first time out of curiosity and fell in love with the magic of a kitchen where my parents' unspoken love existed in abundance, and spoke a thousand words in the language of food.

I never asked my mother a question about stock-making. But I am starting to realize that the time I spent in both my mother's and my maternal grandmother's kitchens taught me fruitful lessons that are now so precious. Not only for remembering the vague methods of how certain dishes were made, but also for the sentiment that allows me to recall the small things and moments, which have become feelings I want to savour.

As I skim off the scum that gathers around the edges of the pan that now smells like an ocean after gentle spring rain, I am softly soothed by the unspoken love of my mother that grew my bones. It makes me wonder if my daughter, with her great sense of smell, will one day know, when the memories of her childhood float back to the blip-blob sound of a simmering stockpot, that I am there with her.

-

Soups and stews are an integral part of Korean meals. We are a nation known to enjoy steaming hot broths to cool down in summer and to warm up in winter. *Si-won-hada* and *gae-un-hada* both indicate 'cooling' or 'refreshing' and describe taste sensations experienced through the body rather than the tongue, regardless of the actual temperature of the dish. The flavours of soups and stews are often talked about, and sought after, with particular need to satisfy these seemingly simple sensations, which are greatly connected to and influenced by the season, mood, weather or, indeed, the occasion.

I do feel so much of Korean food is about observing the harmony between our surroundings, the ingredients and our bodies. And we live by the mantra that food is medicine; therefore to eat well is to live well.

Notes on Types of Korean Soups + Stews

Korean soups and stews can be loosely divided into five types based on the methods of cooking and the ratio of liquid to solid ingredients.

Guk + Tang

These types of soup are texturally thin – usually a lightly seasoned liquid makes up around 70 per cent of the dish, with a small amount of vegetables, meat or fish.

Jjigae

Essentially a stew, this is often served in the middle of the table for everyone to share. It may be worth noting, back when I was growing up, communal eating of shared dishes in the middle of the table with many spoons dipping in and out was a common practice in Korea, as it is considered a good way to bring people closer together.

Jjim

A braised or steamed dish with either no liquid or just a small amount, depending on the ingredient you are cooking with.

Jeongol

A dish in which assorted meat or fish and vegetables are arranged directly into a shallow casserole dish along with seasoning and prepared stock. Not dissimilar to a hotpot, it is typically cooked at the table on a portable stove.

Notes on Keeping Things Do-able

In Korea, soups and stews are usually enjoyed as part of a meal that typically consists of rice and a spread of a few *banchan* dishes. Ordinarily, the assortment isn't lavish but it is thoughtfully arranged

with flavours and seasonal ingredients that balance the whole table. Having a few batch-prepared *banchan* dishes stocked up in the fridge obviously makes life easier.

I also find the simplicity of one soup or stew served with plain steamed rice makes just as delicious an eating experience and is perhaps far more realistic, especially during weekdays when time and headspace are in short supply. Serve it all in one bowl to make it a comforting 'sit in front of the TV' kind of dinner, if you like.

Dishes such as Egg Drop Soup (page 100) and Seaweed Soup with Mussels (page 102) are incredibly quick to make and ideal for a great soothing breakfast. Hearty stew dishes such as Everyday *Doenjang* Stew (page 116), Kimchi Stew with Pork Belly (page 115) and Soft Tofu Stew with Clams (page 118) are all commonly cooked weekday staples in Korean homes, usefully utilizing whatever is in the fridge. You can easily substitute the meat/fish with available ingredients – Korean home cooking is all about being resourceful and versatile! I've tried to take you through the process as clearly as I could, in hope that you will be able to chop and change the suggested proteins or vegetables confidently to suit your locality, your fridge and your preference, so it can become part of your weekly repertoire.

Chicken Soup for the Dog Days (page 111) and Spicy Chicken and Potato Stew (page 110) are fairly straightforward but nonetheless definitely make a triumphant centrepiece for any occasion.

Dishes such as Spicy Pulled Beef Soup (page 105) and Oxtail Soup (page 107) may seem like a daunting task as they are a little time-consuming, but they are mostly hands off. Both dishes produce a handsome yield so are great batch-cooking projects for weekends or on quieter rainy days.

Egg Drop Soup

This egg drop soup very much demonstrates the inherently frugal and adaptable nature of Korean home cooking. At the most basic level, you only need stock and egg with a couple of storecupboard ingredients for seasoning. But when a well-stocked fridge or larder can lend you a bountiful supply of ingredients, it can be bulked up with any vegetables. Eat with a bowl of hot, fluffy steamed rice for a soothing breakfast, or pour over a nest of noodles, and you have a quick and filling meal with scarcely any effort.

Just a few sliced onions provide a little bite and background sweetness. Any other vegetables you wish to use should be added to the soup before the egg so that they are fully cooked by the time you pour in the whisked egg. Thus it might be useful to slice any additional ingredients fairly small so they cook quickly. Some people like to garnish it with chilli but I prefer the warmth of ginger. Soy sauce can be replaced with an equal amount of *doenjang* (Korean fermented bean paste) or even miso, if you fancy a change.

Serves 1–2

For the eggs
2 eggs
2 tsp mirin
½ tsp sea salt flakes
¼ tsp ground white
   pepper

For the stock
550ml (18fl oz/2¼ cups)
   stock of your choice
   (pages 219–221)
1 tbsp soup or light
   soy sauce
1 tbsp mirin
20g (¾oz) onion,
   thinly sliced

To finish
small amount of ginger,
   julienned into thin
   matchsticks
1 spring onion (scallion),
   sliced
a few drops of toasted
   sesame oil

Crack the eggs into a bowl or a small jug with a pouring spout. Season with mirin, salt and white pepper and whisk to combine.

Place the stock of your choice in a saucepan and bring to a gentle simmer over a medium heat. Season with the soy sauce and mirin. Add the sliced onions and simmer for a minute or two so the onions have softened but still have a little bite to them. Check the seasoning and adjust it with salt, if you wish.

Keep the pan on a high simmer, just below boiling point. Hold the whisked eggs in your non-dominant hand, close to the pan. Stir the pan with a chopstick or a spoon in your dominant hand to create a gentle whirlpool and steadily pour in the egg in a circular motion. Don't touch the pan too much once the egg is in. Let the pan come back up to a high simmer. When you see the egg floating back up to the surface, remove from the heat.

To serve, ladle the soup into a bowl and top with some sliced ginger and spring onion. Finish it with a few drops of sesame oil just before serving.

Soups + Stews

Honghap Miyeok Guk

Seaweed Soup with Mussels – or Birthday Soup

This bowl of humble seaweed soup signifies birth. Seaweed, rich in minerals and vitamins, was traditionally given to mothers after a birth for its nutritional benefit. An old wives' tale believed it increased milk production for nursing mothers as well as having healing properties. More traditionally, stock made from dried mussels was given to women for their first meal after labour, instead of more commonly eaten meat-based broths, to avoid any killing of livestock, in order to be respectful to the new life being born.

Tenderly braised seaweed in a delicately flavoured soup celebrates one's mother for their hard labour. It is a small but symbolic gesture to remember the day with gratitude. Korean mothers take great pleasure in offering this soup for birthday breakfast to wish their child a long life in good health; a quiet display of a mother's love, in a Korean way.

The Korean seaweed used in this soup, *miyeok*, is not dissimilar to *wakame*, brown algae commonly associated with Japanese cuisine. More typically, you will see versions with beef stock made from brisket as a base. However, mussels in season are particularly meaty and affordable. I find simple mussel broth not only much quicker to put together, but it also brings a subtly sweet ocean flavour which works really well with naturally salty seaweed.

I have opted to make the mussel broth separately, reserving the meat to add to the soup later. This process allows me to cook the seaweed in the broth for long enough to maximize the flavour of the soup without compromising the texture of the mussels. But by all means, you can simply reserve the mussels in their shells, with the meat still intact, and continue as instructed.

Serves 4

20g (¾oz) *miyeok*
  (Korean seaweed)
500g (1lb 2oz) mussels,
  scrubbed and
  beards removed
1 litre (34fl oz/4 cups)
  just-boiled water
1 tbsp toasted sesame oil
1 tbsp vegetable oil
3 garlic cloves, minced
1 tbsp soup or light
  soy sauce
sea salt flakes, to taste

Soak the *miyeok* in plenty of cold water for 20 minutes. As it absorbs the water, it softens and blooms. Ensure the bowl is big enough to accommodate the volume of rehydrated seaweed.

Discard any mussels that remain open and put the remainder in a large, lidded, heavy-based saucepan, along with the just-boiled water. Bring to the boil, then simmer gently for 10 minutes, or until the shells are opened. Discard any that remain closed. Have a large heatproof bowl or a jug ready and strain the stock through a fine sieve; it will appear translucent milky white. Reserve the stock. Remove the mussels from the shells and set aside. If you choose to keep the meat still intact in their shells, just simply set aside.

Drain the seaweed and squeeze out the excess water. If using pre-cut, set aside. If using uncut, roughly chop it.

Place a lidded, heavy-based saucepan over a low heat. Add both oils to the pan, along with the seaweed. Sauté for 5 minutes, stirring from time to time. The seaweed should darken a little in colour. Stir in the garlic to soften, enough to smell the fragrant aroma.

Pour the reserved mussel broth into the pan. Add the soy sauce. Bring to the boil, then simmer for 30 minutes. Add the reserved mussel meat and cook for 5 minutes to gently warm through. Remove from the heat. Check the seasoning and adjust with a touch more salt, if needed. Divide the soup into four bowls and serve with plain steamed rice.

<u>**SOUPS**</u>

Spicy Pulled Beef Soup

Yukgaejang

This spicy beef soup begins by creating a base stock with meat gently simmered in an aromatic bath. Cooked meat pieces are then hand shredded and marinated in a spicy seasoning along with blanched vegetables that typically include dried fernbrake, taro stem, sweet potato stem, beansprouts and/or Korean spring onion. This dish, in particular, really benefits from the slow process that respects the traditional method of handling each ingredient separately. In return, it ensures the harmonious infusion of flavours and textures you can distinguish, both individually but also together.

Korean food isn't widely known as regional, but the way each dish is prepared and the final balance of seasoning, changes dramatically as you travel, with locals adopting ingredients more common to their area. In Seoul, the beef is more often cooked with bones to make the stock richer and meatier, and the meat more flavoursome. True Seoul-style soup is also often made with only Korean spring onion as the chosen vegetable, which contributes natural sweetness and clean-tasting depth. Korean spring onion, called *daepa*, is much bigger than its Western counterpart. It perhaps looks more like a leek, although tastes quite different: the white parts taste quite oniony and fragrant, while the green parts are a little punchier. I opt for a mixture of leek and spring onion here, to create a fair representation of the dish and a good balance of allium flavour.

Don't let the time-consuming aspect put you off. Once you get the hang of the process, and the most hands-on part, it is quite straightforward to bring together.

Pat the beef dry with kitchen paper to remove any sitting blood. Cut the beef into 6cm (2¼in) long chunks, ensuring the grain runs evenly lengthways. Place the beef in a large stockpot, along with the daikon radish, leek, onion, *dasima* and black peppercorns. Top with the water and bring to the boil. You will notice some scum rising to the surface as the water reaches boiling point. Skim off but don't worry too much – it will all sort itself out as it simmers. Lower the heat immediately and maintain a low simmer with small bubbles rising intermittently. Cook for 2½ hours with the lid ajar, or until tender, but remove the *dasima* after 1 hour.

The meat doesn't need to be fork tender but tender enough to hand shred into chunky pieces. Remove the meat and set aside to cool. When the stock has cooled a little, carefully pass the beef stock through the strainer into a heatproof jug or directly into the heavy-based, lidded pan you will be cooking the soup in. Measure out 1.2 litres (40fl oz/4¾ cups) of stock and reserve – I do this by weighing the liquid as I pour the stock through the strainer. Save any leftover stock for another time. Discard the solids.

Meanwhile, bring a pan of salted water to the boil. Blanch the leeks very briefly to wilt. Rinse under cold water, drain well and set aside. Blanch the beansprouts in the same water for 3 minutes so they are floppy and softened. Rinse under cold water and drain. Squeeze the water out quite firmly and set aside.

Put the vegetable oil and *gochugaru* for the seasoning into a small, cold saucepan.

→

Serves 6

250g (9oz) leeks, white parts only, halved and sliced into 5cm (2in) batons
300g (10½oz) beansprouts
6 spring onions (scallions), cut into 5cm (2in) batons
sea salt flakes, to season

For the stock
450g (1lb) beef (a mixture of bavette and shin or brisket)
200g (7oz) daikon radish, cut into large chunks
1 leek, cut in half crossways
½ onion, cleaned with skin left on
five 5 × 7.5cm (2 × 3in) sheets of *dasima* (dried kelp)
1 tbsp black peppercorns
2.5 litres (85fl oz/10½ cups) water

For the seasoning
3 tbsp vegetable oil
4 tbsp finely ground *gochugaru* (Korean red pepper flakes)
2 tbsp mirin
2 tbsp soy sauce
2 tbsp soup or light soy sauce
1 tbsp toasted sesame oil
2 tbsp fish sauce
½ tsp freshly cracked black pepper
30g (1oz) garlic cloves, minced

Place it over a low heat to gently warm up the oil. As it warms up, the *gochugaru* will start to bloom. Stir constantly to move the *gochugaru* around to stop it from burning. You will notice the flakes starts to swell and become more like an oily paste. It will start to smell very fragrant and feel almost aerated. This takes about 4 minutes total. Remove from the heat. Transfer to a large heatproof mixing bowl and add the mirin, both soy sauces, the sesame oil, fish sauce, ground pepper and garlic. Give it a good stir and set aside.

When the meat has cooled down enough to handle, shred it lengthways into fairly chunky pieces using two forks or your hands. Add the meat to the mixing bowl above, along with the blanched leeks and beansprouts. Wear gloves to toss everything together by hand to combine, gently massaging and pinching the ingredients – I think the warmth of your fingers and gentle pressure of hands really help to coat every bit of meat and vegetable more harmoniously.

To bring the dish together, transfer the seasoned meat and vegetables into a large, heavy-based, lidded pan along with the 1.2 litres of reserved beef stock. Place the pan over a high heat to bring it up to the boil with the lid on, then immediately lower the heat to simmer for 35 minutes or so with the lid on ajar. Check the seasoning and adjust with salt (about ½ teaspoon), if needed. You want to taste the sort of heat that gently tickles the back of the throat, with a touch of mellow sweetness that comes from the leeks. Add the spring onions and simmer for a further 10 minutes.

When ready, divide the soup into deep soup bowls and serve immediately while steaming hot with plain steamed rice.

Oxtail Soup

You may have heard of a dish called *seolleongtang*: more commonly known as milky white Korean beef bone soup. *Gomtang* is not dissimilar, except it uses a generous amount of meat such as brisket, shin, ribs and tail to flavour the broth, instead of relying solely on bones. Thus the broth usually appears clearer than the former, although nowadays, the difference between the two is often minimal as both use more meat or bones to enhance the flavour of the soup, as I do here.

Using oxtail alone, it is difficult to achieve the rich milky white broth. I rely on the addition of beef stock bones to rectify this problem, which allows me to take the bone broth as far as necessary to yield the creamy richness that gives an almost nutty undertone. Oxtail meat in this dish should be tender but still retain a pleasantly bouncy and gelatinous chew that translates as *jjolgithada*: one of many expressions that describes Korea's much-treasured texture of food in your mouth.

Traditionally, this dish is often served with a side of ripe Cubed Daikon Radish Kimchi (page 79). Well-fermented kimchi has a pleasant sourness that complements the clean-tasting broth. The dipping sauce for the meat here lends a good level of acidity, which works so well in the absence of radish kimchi.

The process isn't too difficult, although it is a little time-consuming and requires patience. Begin the process at least one day in advance; preferably two.

Place the beef bones (not the oxtail) in a large bowl and submerge completely in plenty of cold water for 2 hours, changing the water after the first hour. You will notice blood in the water. In Korea, blood in meat bones results in an unpleasant odour to the finished dish and letting the blood out is an important step which ensures a clean-tasting soup. After 2 hours, rinse the bones thoroughly under cold running water, then drain.

Pat the oxtail pieces dry with kitchen paper to remove the sitting blood, if any. Place the oxtail pieces in a large stockpot, along with the beef bones. Fill it with cold water and bring to a rapid boil, uncovered. You will notice a foamy brown scum appears on the surface after about 10–12 minutes. Remove from the heat. Carefully drain the water out and rinse the oxtail and bones under cold water, ensuring they are clean and free of any scum. Drain.

Trim the excess fat from the oxtail with kitchen scissors. Set aside.

Clean the stockpot thoroughly. Put the oxtail and bones back into the stockpot and fill it with about 3 litres (100fl oz/12 cups) of water to submerge everything. Bring to the boil uncovered and skim off any scum, then simmer over a low–medium heat for 4 hours, with the lid left on ajar. Check occasionally to skim off the fat. Top up with just-boiled water every so often to ensure everything remains submerged throughout. You should be able to hear your simmering pot and be able to see the intermittently rising bubbles. The heat shouldn't be so ferocious that it thrashes the bones about too much but not so low that you can't see the bubbles.

After 4 hours, you will notice that the oxtail meat has just started to pull away from the bones.

→

Serves 4

For the soup
1kg (2lb 4oz) mixture of
   beef stock bones and
   marrow bones
1kg (2lb 4oz) oxtail

For the meat dipping sauce
2 tbsp soy sauce
2 tbsp rice vinegar
2 tbsp water
1 tsp golden granulated
   sugar
1 tsp *gochugaru* (Korean
   red pepper flakes)
1 tsp toasted sesame oil
1 spring onion (scallion),
   finely chopped
1 garlic clove, finely
   minced
¼ small red onion,
   thinly sliced and
   soaked in cold water
   for 10 minutes

To finish
sea salt flakes, to season
3 spring onions
   (scallions), white parts
   only, sliced
2 garlic cloves, minced
freshly cracked black
   pepper, to season

SOUPS

Remove the oxtail, cool and refrigerate until needed. Continue simmering the rest of the mixed bones for a further 2 hours, then turn off the heat. Remove the remaining bones from the pot using a wire skimmer – reserve the bones if you wish to continue with the second boiling (see notes). If you decide not to, which is perfectly okay, discard the bones.

Let the broth cool down before carefully pouring it into a heatproof container (you should have about 1 litre (34fl oz/4 cups). Refrigerate the batch to cool completely, preferably overnight. You will notice the next morning that the stock has now set and any fat has hardened enough to skim off – do this.

To bring the dish together, combine the bone broth and reserved oxtail pieces (both batches of bone broth, if you did the second boil) in a heavy-based saucepan. Simmer gently for 20 minutes.

Meanwhile, mix all the ingredients for the dipping sauce in a bowl. Set side.

(If you used both batches of bone broth, at this stage ladle half the liquid into a heatproof container and store in the fridge for another use.) Taste and season the soup with salt just before serving. Divide the oxtail pieces between four bowls and ladle the soup over the meat. Top with a generous amount of sliced spring onion and a little minced garlic. Serve the dipping sauce and black pepper on the side. Eat while steaming hot with plain steamed rice or thin wheat noodles.

NOTES ON SECOND BOIL

-

You can decide whether you would like to continue with the second boil of the mixed bones (not the oxtail). In Korea, it is common to reboil the bones up to three times, and it is believed that the second batch yields a slightly tastier broth. I occasionally do a second boil on the following day, repeating the process of boiling for another 4 hours with the bones submerged in about 4 litres (135fl oz/16½ cups) of water. After the second boil has finished, remove and discard the bones. Let the second batch of broth cool down completely, then store in the fridge. Skim off the hardened fat the next day.

Spicy Chicken + Potato Stew

This Korean chicken stew is every bit of my childhood home 5,000 miles away and my home here in London, eaten whenever the familiar comfort of heat is required. And if you are like me and believe that the most immediate relief of stress can come from the glowing warmth of chilli, this dish is definitely for you.

The heat comes from both *gochujang* and *gochugaru*, with the former providing the umami rich heat that carries the salty-sweet undertone, while the latter contributes the fruity foreground chilli kick. And whilst the dish might sound spicy, it is neither the blow-your-face-off sort of hot nor tongue-numbingly fiery, and lends a wonderful sweetness that I would like to think you will be able to enjoy pleasantly, providing you have a decent level of tolerance to chilli. The level of spiciness offered, especially in *gochujang*, will be greatly different from brand to brand, so be mindful.

Cut both carrots and potatoes chunky to help them retain their shape better, so that they are not completely lost in the stew. Fluffy potatoes crumble buttery soft in the mouth and naturally thicken the gravy. The tenderness of potatoes here is a clear winner that is especially delicious, bound with the sauce over plain white steamed rice. If such a thing as Korean curry ever existed, this would be it.

Serves 4 generously

For the chicken
2 tbsp *gochugaru* (Korean red pepper flakes)
2 tbsp soy sauce
2 tbsp mirin
1 tbsp toasted sesame oil
1½ tbsp *gochujang* (Korean red chilli paste)
2 tsp golden granulated sugar
4 garlic cloves, minced
2 tsp thin julienne matchsticks of ginger root
½ tsp freshly cracked black pepper
8 chicken thighs, on the bone without skin

For the stew
1 tbsp vegetable oil
2 tsp crushed chilli
½ large or 1 small onion, sliced
800ml (28fl oz/1½ cups) just-boiled water
2 carrots, cut into large chunks
4 small potatoes, cut into large chunks
2 tsp fish sauce
sea salt flakes to season

To finish
1 spring onion (scallion), thinly sliced diagonally
toasted white sesame seeds

In a large mixing bowl, combine the *gochugaru*, soy sauce, mirin, sesame oil, *gochujang*, sugar, garlic, ginger and black pepper. Add the chicken thighs and massage thoroughly to coat the chickens with sauce. Set aside.

Place the vegetable oil and crushed chilli in a large, heavy-based, lidded casserole dish or saucepan, and warm up gently over a medium heat. In a few minutes, you will notice the red from the chilli flakes start to bleed into the oil, making the oil appear coppery red. Add the onions and sauté gently for a few minutes until the onions soften a little and the edges start to catch a touch of colour. Stir occasionally.

Add the chicken to the pan and briefly stir to combine, before carefully pouring in the just-boiled water. You may want to rinse the mixing bowl with a little water to scrape in the remaining bits of sauce. Increase the heat to bring the stew to bubble, then turn the heat down to simmer for 15 minutes.

Add the carrot and potato chunks. Put the lid on ajar and simmer gently for a further 35 minutes.

By now, the chicken should be tender, almost falling off the bones. Add the fish sauce and adjust the seasoning with salt, if necessary. The gravy should taste glowingly spicy with a little background sweetness and deep umami saltiness. Some may prefer the dish on the sweeter side, so do feel free to add a touch more sugar, if you wish.

To serve, divide the stew between four bowls, with one or two chicken thighs per person. Or serve the dish as a centrepiece, family style, so everyone can help themselves. Top with spring onion and a little pinch of sesame seeds. Eat with plain steamed rice.

Chicken Soup for the Dog Days

Dak Baeksuk

I don't know about you but chicken soup for me feels like a universal language of home comfort that brings a warm glow to the soul; a real feel-good food.

Boiled chicken soup is one of the dishes directly associated with *sambok* culture in Korea, which is celebrated during the summer in three important events during the hottest part of the year, usually between July and August. *Chobok* indicates the first ten days of summer, followed by *jungbok*, the hottest 20 days of summer in the middle, and then *malbok*, the beginning of the final ten hot days of summer. It is believed that during *sambok* the smooth functioning of our bodies is compromised due to rising heat, causing weakening of the digestion, loss of energy and tiredness. Hot soups are often eaten to restore the warm energy to our internal body in an effort to restore the balance. It is hardly surprising that, for many, chicken soup has always been a firm favourite for the occasion.

Baeksuk uses mature chicken to flavour the soup. It is always cooked unsalted and more typically without the addition of ginseng or other medicinal barks and roots (which are often used in another common type of chicken soup called *samgyetang*). The dish is typically eaten with a thick rice porridge (Mung Bean Porridge – page 176) made with the reserved stock to bolster the spread afterwards, though I sometimes much prefer to enjoy the soup simply with a bowl of rice on the side, saving the pleasure of making the porridge for breakfast the next day.

Please do serve the chicken whole in family style, with the dipping salt, so that everyone can get their hands (or tongs) in to pick the bits they like. It pairs well with Cut Cabbage Kimchi (page 75) or Cubed Daikon Radish Kimchi (page 79).

Place the onion, garlic, leek and ginger in a large, lidded stockpot and add the water. Bring to the boil, then simmer gently for 20 minutes. Carefully scoop out the vegetables, using a fine sieve, and discard.

Trim any excess fat off the chicken and remove the parson's nose. Add the chicken to the pan, breast-side down; you may need to top with some hot water to submerge the chicken completely. Bring to the boil, then simmer for 10 minutes over a medium heat with the lid on ajar. Then reduce the heat again to maintain a gentle simmer and cook for a further 35–40 minutes over a low heat with the lid on, until cooked through. When the meat has pulled away from the legs, it's a sure sign it is cooked through. If the chicken requires further cooking, just continue simmering until it is done.

When ready, turn off the heat and rest the chicken in the stock for 10 minutes before serving.

While the chicken is cooking, make the dipping sauce by pounding the garlic with the salt in a pestle and mortar to make a paste. Mix in the sesame oil and black pepper. Stir well and set aside.

Transfer the whole chicken to a large rimmed dish, deep enough to comfortably house some of the soup too, so that everyone can help themselves. Scatter the sesame seeds on top. Serve the garnish of spring onion and garlic on the side, so people can take what they want to flavour their soup. Serve with the dipping sauce for the meat, and a small bowl of sea salt flakes for seasoning the soup.

Pictured overleaf.

Serves 4

1 onion, sliced in half
  with skin left on
1 whole bulb of
  garlic, peeled
1 leek, cut in half
2 tsp thickly sliced
  ginger root
3 litres (100fl oz/12 cups)
  water
1 large chicken, weighing
  about 1.5kg (3lb 5oz)

For the dipping sauce
1 garlic clove, finely minced
2 tsp sea salt flakes
2 tbsp toasted sesame oil
½ tsp freshly cracked
  black pepper

To finish
1 tsp toasted sesame
  seeds, lightly crushed
3 spring onions (scallions),
  thinly sliced
2 garlic cloves, finely
  minced
sea salt flakes, to season

Kimchi Stew with Pork Belly

Kimchi Jjigae

Well-aged kimchi carries a depth of acidity that is often too sour to consume in its raw state, but is prized for its ability to cut through the fattiness of pork belly. Its pronounced, pungent flavour complements the richness of pork beautifully. The lacklustre texture of old kimchi is greatly improved by gentle sautéing in a little oil with the addition of sugar that balances the sourness. Don't be tempted to caramelize it too far, as when *gochugaru* burns, it tastes unpleasantly bitter: we're here to soften, not to caramelize.

I don't bother removing the pork skin as I don't mind the gelatinous texture of skin in this stew; but feel free to remove it, if you wish. There are contrasting opinions on whether to brown the meat before adding it to the kimchi. I personally think the meat retains moisture better and is more tender when only briefly stirred in, simply combined with sautéed kimchi.

Kimchi *jjigae* should not be limp; instead it should have the vigour and tanginess that linger enough to make you salivate spoon after spoon. The final seasoning of the dish will greatly depend on the quality and ripeness of the kimchi you're using. Try adding a touch of vinegar right at the end, to give the dish an uplifting sour note.

Heat both the vegetable and sesame oils in a large, lidded, heavy-based saucepan. Add the onion and sauté over a medium heat for a few minutes to soften and start to colour a little, then turn down the heat a touch and add the kimchi, garlic, sugar and *gochugaru*. Cook gently for a good 10 minutes, stirring occasionally. It will start to smell very fragrant and the kimchi will appear softened and quite a bit darker in colour.

Stir in the pork belly and mirin, then pour in the water. Stir in the *doenjang*, *gochujang* and shrimp paste. Crank up the heat to bring it to the boil. Once it starts to bubble, reduce the heat and simmer gently for 40 minutes with the lid on ajar.

By now, the pork should be very tender and the broth rich and unctuous. Add the tofu. Check for seasoning and adjust it with a pinch more salt, if necessary. Continue to simmer with the lid on for 10 minutes until the tofu has softened to absorb the flavour. Taste and stir in the vinegar, if using, before removing from the heat.

Divide the stew into four deep bowls. Top with spring onion and crushed sesame seeds. Serve immediately while steaming hot, with plain steamed rice.

Serves 4

1 tbsp vegetable oil
1 tbsp toasted sesame oil
½ onion, thinly sliced
350g (12oz) overripe kimchi, roughly chopped
3 garlic cloves, minced
1 tsp golden granulated sugar
1½ tbsp *gochugaru* (Korean red pepper flakes)
300g (10½oz) pork belly, cubed into bite-size pieces (skin removed, if desired)
1 tbsp mirin
1 litre (34fl oz/4 cups) water
2 tsp *doenjang* (Korean fermented bean paste)
1 tsp *gochujang* (Korean red chilli paste)
1 tsp shrimp paste
250g (9oz) firm tofu, cubed
sea salt flakes, to season
1 tbsp brown rice vinegar (optional)

For the garnish
2 spring onions (scallions), thinly sliced
½ tsp toasted white sesame seeds, lightly crushed

Everyday *Doenjang* Stew

Deeply umami-rich *doenjang* (Korean fermented soybean paste) gives this dish a wonderfully earthy depth, while odds and ends of vegetables provide a gentle background sweetness. It's a humble and honest dish, which perfectly demonstrates the frugal nature of Korean home cooking.

Transitioning fluidly from season to season, in summer, tender courgettes and early green chillies take centre stage. Courgettes are softened just enough to provide the stew with a delicate sweetness and lightness, while young peppery green chillies add a contrasting fresh bite. Autumn is for warmth: the glut of earthy mushrooms or sweet squash will do a fine job, taking the stew into the richer side, especially with the addition of meat protein, if you like. I particularly enjoy thinly sliced bavette steak, which can be sautéed in a little sesame oil before adding the stock, or wonderfully sweet and salty clams added towards the end of cooking to bring briny umami. And as we enter a long, cold winter, we rely on the heartier root vegetables that are in abundance until the warmth of spring gently breaks the earth to bring wild foraged bitter greens and peppery leaves to revitalize our sleepy palates.

Cooking the onions and potatoes first allows the stock to take on a subtle sweetness; starch from the potatoes will help to thicken the stew slightly too. Add the courgettes and mushrooms later as they require less cooking time. If you're using different vegetables, do keep this in mind and adjust the order accordingly.

Serves 4

½ onion, diced
150g (5oz) potatoes, cut into bite-size chunks
900ml (32fl oz/3¾ cups) stock of your choice (pages 219–221)
3 garlic cloves, minced
3 tbsp *doenjang* (Korean fermented bean paste)
2 tsp *gochujang* (Korean red chilli paste)
1 tsp *gochugaru* (Korean red pepper flakes)
200g (7oz) courgettes (zucchini), quartered and cut into bite-size chunks
200g (7oz) tofu, cut into bite-size cubes
75g (½oz) mushrooms (shimeji, enoki or shiitake)
sea salt flakes, to taste
2 mild or hot green chillies, sliced
2 spring onions (scallions), sliced

Put the onions and potatoes into a lidded, heavy-based saucepan, along with the stock. Put the lid on ajar and bring the stock up to a gentle simmer, then cook for 10 minutes over a low heat until the onions are soft and the potatoes are almost cooked through.

Add the garlic and stir in the *doenjang*, *gochujang* and *gochugaru*. Add the courgettes and tofu. If the mushrooms need cooking for longer than a few minutes, add them now. Enoki mushrooms can be added right at the end, as they only need a minute or two to cook.

Increase the heat to medium so you can see the stock bubbling. Simmer for 15 minutes, or until the tofu has absorbed the flavour and the courgettes have softened. Check for seasoning and adjust it with a pinch more salt, if necessary. Add the green chillies and most of the spring onions. Cook for a further 2 minutes.

Divide the stew into four bowls. Top with the reserved spring onion and serve immediately while steaming hot, with steamed rice.

Bajirak
Soondubu Jjigae

Soft Tofu Stew with Clams

When I was pregnant with my daughter, I took an overnight train from Seoul to Jeoung Dong Jin, a quiet coastal town known for its breathtaking sunrise. The train was crowded and occasionally loud with the excitement of youth. Unable to fall asleep sitting upright, I leant my head against my husband's shoulder, with my eyes vacantly staring out at the dark, hoping for some refuge. My pregnant body was jet-lagged, uncomfortable and unable to rest, but eager to see the sun rising from the ocean, as if it was a promise of something good and bright for the unknown future I feared as a new mother-to-be. I always felt comforted by the blistering sea. When the wind from the ocean is strong enough to slap me in the face, the very discomfort makes me feel wide awake and more in tune with my surroundings. To feel the fear was to be alive for me, and the depth of the sea always made me feel grateful for life.

I'd been here before as a young and naïve youth seeking answers in solitude. A quaint train station sat right behind the pine-tree-lined sandy beach and ocean, with one of its platforms directly overlooking the sea. Standing amongst the crowd, I watched the golden sun rise slowly from the horizon and paint the sky a burning amber red. It was breathtakingly beautiful and made my bone-deep, cold, shivering flesh melt away in awe at the beauty beyond what I could behold. It gave me hope – both back when I was a girl and now as a woman bearing a child.

It was here that I ate this soft tofu stew for breakfast. I have eaten this stew many times before but here, in an area famous for soft tofu made with water from the eastern sea, it tasted different. Soft tofu stew came bubbling hot in its earthenware pot, carefully rested on top of a wooden tray. Barely cooked egg sat cracked in the middle. Deep, fiery-red stew was much like the impressive sunrise. I took the first mouthful impatiently, almost burning the roof of my mouth but oblivious nonetheless, slurping away the soft, custard-like creamy tofu. It tastes nothing much other than mildly nutty, then its nothingness starts to shine, providing much-needed relief from the hot broth, both in its temperature and spiciness. I broke into the barely cooked egg yolk to temper the heat of the chilli. The golden liquid oozed into the soup, now gloriously luscious and creamy amongst salty and briny clams, heavenly drunk in the pool of spicy pork fat. The broth tasted deeply rich and velvety, warming and comforting. And the dish still to me feels like the promise of hope for something good.

Serves 2

1 tbsp *gochu giruem* (chilli oil)
1 tbsp vegetable oil
100g (3½oz) minced (ground) pork
1 tbsp toasted sesame oil
½ onion, thinly sliced
3 garlic cloves, minced
½ tsp grated ginger root
1½ tbsp *gochugaru* (Korean red pepper flakes)
1 tbsp mirin
400ml (13fl oz/generous 1½ cups) stock of your choice (pages 219–221)
1 tbsp + 1 tsp soup or light soy sauce
1 tbsp fish sauce
¼ tsp ground white pepper
120g (4oz) courgettes (zucchini), quartered and sliced
200g (7oz) clams, cleaned and purged if necessary
1 × 300g (10½oz) pack of soft (silken) tofu
40g (1½oz) enoki mushrooms
½ tsp sea salt flakes, or to taste

To finish
2 eggs, whole or just yolks (optional)
1 green finger chilli, chopped
1 spring onion (scallion), thinly sliced

Heat the chilli oil and vegetable oil in a heavy-based saucepan. Add the pork and fry over a medium heat until deep golden brown, stirring energetically every now and then. It should take about 3 minutes, after which it will start to make a popping sound and catch a little on the bottom of the pan.

Lower the heat immediately. Add the sesame oil to the pan along with the onion, garlic and ginger, with a good pinch of salt. Sauté gently, stirring occasionally, until the onions are softened a little and it starts to smell fragrant. Add the *gochugaru* and stir constantly for a minute without letting it burn. You will notice the onions and the oils turn red.

Add the mirin. Pour in the stock and stir in the soy sauce, fish sauce and white pepper. Add the courgettes, clams and soft tofu. Roughly break up the tofu with a spoon and increase the heat to bring to the boil. Once it starts to bubble rapidly, reduce the heat to medium and cook for 10 minutes or so until the courgettes are tender and the clams cooked through. Discard any clams that remain closed. Adjust the seasoning with salt. Scatter with the enoki mushrooms and gently crack in the eggs, if using. Scatter with chopped green chillies and cover with a lid to steam the eggs for a minute or two.

Divide the stew between two bowls, carefully scooping each egg into the bowl. Or serve it family style: directly from the pan in the middle of the table. Top with spring onion and serve immediately while steaming hot, with plain steamed rice.

Meat

four

the poor in me wants to gorge on the meat

Our late dinner outings almost always ended up in the same small restaurant tucked well away from the main road, positioned in the corner of a relatively quiet local market. The place was well known to the locals but otherwise a well-kept secret. Only those who chased flavours with a discerning palate would come here for its famous *dwaeji galbi* (soy marinated pork ribs).

It often made me wonder how my father managed to find these places. He knew all the best places to eat: places known for particular dishes, often hidden away and unassuming restaurants that most people would just pass by without noticing.

The restaurant was always heaving and the room was perfumed heavily with charcoal smoke from the juices of sweet soy marinade hitting the sizzling white-hot coals. The juices dripped down to sweat the charcoals underneath, turning it to glow red and amber. The smoke was intense but also delicious. It hit my eyes and blinded my senses. It laced our hair and stained our lips.

We sat by the open window. There were uncles lighting coals and cleaning grill grates, with cigarettes behind their ears. Flecks of fire fluttered around the streets flooded with neon lights like fireflies. Fizzy lemonade bubbles tingled my nose. Cold and fresh blue air skimmed my happy face, breaking the space between the smoke and clinking noises in and out of the room. People moved quickly and the energy was electric. The ladies, called aunties, serving tables rushed around and diners called for help with waving hands and cheerful sound of '*Yeogiyo!*' to grab the attention of one of them. The aunties moved from table to table to pull down the extractor fans from the ceiling and place them closer to the grills to suck up the fumes. And I watched them in awe as they skilfully turned and cut the meat with tongs and scissors as if they were an extension of their own limbs.

The meat tasted salty-sweet with a caramel-like scent. The slightly overdone crispy ends had the flavours of intensely rich muscovado sugar. Dipped in salty umami-rich *ssamjang*, I positioned it purposefully atop the rusty red-freckled green leaf, while carefully scanning the table to seek out the tart, pickled mooli salad to place on top to balance out the chilli heat. I remember how that felt in my mouth: cold and crunchy and hot and sweet all at once. The *ssam* was always bigger than my mouth could handle and my greediness for a good balance of flavour was evident, with juices dripping down my chin. My hands were covered in a sticky wet mess but I was glad to lick them clean, all the while planning my next bite, my eyes gazing at minty perilla leaves and a *gochugaru*-speckled fresh spring onion salad.

My father ordered enough meat to feed two families and then some, and slurped icy *donchimi* broth, shoving the meaty ribs to the outer corner of the sticky grill for later. The ice-cold, slushy-like radish-water kimchi broth tasted sweeter than my mother's, and ever so slightly effervescent from the fermentation. None of us bothered with it, except my father who would drink the whole jugful twice and claim, '*Ah, siwonhada!*' – a Korean expression meaning 'refreshing' – a taste sensation experienced through the body rather than just received by the tongue.

'The poor in me wants to gorge on the meat' was often what I thought about my father. Born into a poor home as the eldest of four, growing up with very little food around him, he knew what it meant to be hungry and what it meant to be able to afford food, and he wanted to do that well when he was finally able to. He searched out and chased down good food and made sure his appetite for something delicious was suitably rewarded. For him, both quality and quantity – in the sense of generosity – mattered a great deal.

I still remember how the rising smoke made my eyes water with happiness and how sweet that lime-flavoured lemonade tasted. Our faces glowed warm and the smell of charcoal lingered for days to remind me of the food I had eaten. My rose-tinted love and affection for grilling meat over hot charcoal at the table continues, and I am forever allured by the sweet scent of caramelizing soy sauce and smoke that instantly takes me back to the familiar tastes of my childhood. It makes me wonder if my daughter will ever remember the same feelings when she smells the barbecue. Will she recall that these ordinary days are what pieced her childhood together?

-

I have divided this meat chapter into two segments: recipes that use the grilling technique in one, and another which demonstrates the other cooking techniques. Most of the recipes will benefit from the accompaniment of *ssam* and a few *banchan* dishes on the side, in which case I have made suggestions for dishes that may go well with the main affair.

NOTES ON KOREAN BARBECUE

In Korea, restaurants offering table barbecue are everywhere and generally affordable. Typically, thinly sliced meat is cooked over a charcoal or a gas grill built into the table itself. If such an option is not available, a portable stove is offered, so that everyone can still get involved. Meat tends to be prepared in two ways,

depending on the cut being used – either marinated wet to tenderize and add further flavour, or simply seasoned and/or cured to capture the true taste of the chosen cut.

After many trials and errors trying to recreate the Korean barbecue experience at home here in London, I have, however, come to the conclusion that the use of thinly sliced meat is not necessary or even preferable, as most of us tend to grill our meat in the garden and serve it once the cooking is finished, as opposed to cooking it as we dine. The only reasons to use thinly sliced meat, as far as I can tell, are a) to cook it quickly as you go, as cooked-through meat is traditionally preferred, and b) when eating with chopsticks, most cuts need to be of a manageable size, hence bigger pieces of meat are often further diced with tongs and scissors upon cooking. For that reason, tongs and scissors are the most common utensils of choice when it comes to table barbecue.

So, with this in mind, I would suggest you think of Korean barbecue as simply a way of enjoying meat – a culture rather than a singular or particular dish. Choose a cut of meat you like, marinate or prepare it using the recipes here as a guide, and then you can build upon and accompany them with the other elements of the Korean barbecue table to create your own version of this sensory experience.

NOTES ON ACCOMPANIMENTS

On *Ssam + Ssamjang*

At the most basic level, the Korean barbecue experience should be accompanied by *ssam* and *ssamjang*. *Ssam*, which translates as 'wrapped', describes the way in which you wrap a piece of meat – or other fillings – with either raw or blanched leafy vegetables. Think seasonal leaves that are suitable for wrapping, and consider incorporating different textures and tastes, such as sweet, grassy/herby, bitter, juicy, tender or crunchy. I like to use a mixture of soft, sweet lettuce and bitter leaves together for contrast. Perilla leaves are a common addition and great for adding a herbaceous flavour if you can find them. Japanese shiso is also good. Otherwise, try other soft herbs such as mint or basil instead. Blanched white cabbage is a firm favourite in our household as it is sweet and juicy with a perfectly neutral taste that can support both bold and delicate flavours.

Ready-made *ssamjang* is widely available from Asian grocers and perfectly fine, although I do think it is much nicer when you make your own, using a mixture of *doenjang* and *gochujang*, as you can balance the flavours to suit your palate. I have shared a recipe for *Ssamjang* (page 222) which uses blackstrap molasses and a touch of vinegar to bring rounder sweetness and acidity to cut through the richness of the meat.

NOTES ON *BANCHAN*

Banchan dishes are a nice addition which help to balance out an otherwise meat-heavy meal. Kimchi is an easy, go-to small dish which you may have already if you have batched in advance. It is especially great when fermented just right as it will bring a refreshing tanginess. Try grilling kimchi with meat. It is particularly good with pork, as the rendered fat of pork changes the tone of the kimchi from loud and sharp around the edges to mellow and silky, as though you have stir-fried it in the most delicious butter.

Be mindful of the marinade and the type of meat you're preparing when deciding which *banchan* dishes you want to add to the table. Think different textures, colours and flavours. For instance, a rich, wet marinade may call for a side of light and tart *banchan* to bring freshness. Whereas dry-cured or simply seasoned meat may be better paired with saucier *banchan*.

What I find helpful in order to build a flavourful table is to work on five basic taste profiles – salty, sweet, spicy, sour and bitter – and include dishes that provide some or all of these elements so the overall flavour and texture of the meal is balanced.

NOTES ON *JJIGAE*

Most Korean barbecue ends with a shared *jjigae*, which is typically served bubbling hot in an earthenware pot. Commonly, this is Everyday *Doenjang* Stew (page 116) studded with a few finely cubed seasonal vegetables and tofu, and served with a bowl of rice. However, it isn't uncommon to be served a simple bowl of soup to accompany the rice instead. For me though, rice and *jjigae* aren't always needed, so don't feel restricted by the customary rules. This is an option for you to consider.

NOTES ON NOODLES

Sometimes, a bowl of noodles – especially a cold variety – may be preferred at the end of the meal. This is particularly great on hot days, as they are cooling and refreshing. Good choices are cold Buckwheat Noodles in Icy Pink Broth (page 184) or Spicy Cold Noodles (page 188). It isn't uncommon to share a bowl or two across the table.

Once again, I do think there are times where a decent spread of meat with a simple selection of seasonal leafy vegetables for *ssam* is really enough, and sometimes this can be a much more effective way of enjoying the experience. So keep it simple, focus on the key elements and have fun with your barbecue.

OTHER CONDIMENTS

Along with *ssam* and *ssamjang*, a few other condiments are usually offered to complement the grilled meat. I have listed these here so that you can easily locate and prepare them.

Konggaru (Roasted Soybean Powder)

Traditionally this is served with Roasted Pork Belly (page

140), which gives the meat a wonderful nuttiness. You can find it in Asian grocers or health food stores. It is best stored in the fridge in an airtight container as it quickly loses its nutty aroma when stored at room temperature.

Sogeumjang + Gireumjang (Sesame Oil + Salt Dipping Sauce)

This is mostly served with grilled meat where the meat is not marinated in liquid. The mixture of sesame oil and salt provides a buttery nuttiness and additional seasoning, and the inclusion of finely ground black pepper is also common practice. Sometimes sesame oil is omitted when serving beef, however, as some people believe the strong fragrance and taste of sesame oil can overwhelm the true taste of beef. As a general rule, I like a ratio of three parts oil to one part slightly ground down flaky salt with a liberal amount of black pepper.

Yangpa Jeorim (Onion Salad with Wasabi Soy Vinaigrette)

This simple salad is known to many as one of the best accompaniments for any grilled meat, along with the Spring Onion Salad (see right). It is served in individual rimmed plates and acts like a dipping sauce: you dip the meat in the dressing and eat a few slices of onion and meat together. Thinly sliced onion is lightly pickled with a tart dressing of soy vinaigrette spiked with wasabi. Depending on the season, garlic chives may be used instead of onion, or you can simply use chives. Typically it is made with brown Spanish onions but I do like to use red onion or sweet varieties when they're in season.

Soak your sliced onions in cold water for a good 15 minutes to remove the strong taste. The dressing is simply made using more or less equal parts of soy sauce, vinegar, sugar and water. I like to use light soy sauce for this to keep the overall colour of the dressing less dark. For me, cider vinegar is preferable for its tartness, but you can also use rice vinegar. Mix in wasabi paste to taste. I prefer to use wasabi powder made into a paste and I add about ½ tsp of this to a dressing made up of 1 tbsp each of soy sauce, vinegar, sugar and water mixture, depending on the strength of wasabi paste. The overall taste of the dressing should be refreshingly tart, balanced with sweetness and subtle salinity. The heat of wasabi should be present to make your nose tingle a little, which will add to the refreshing sensation but not be overpoweringly spicy.

Pajeori Pa Muchim (Spring Onion Salad)

An essential accompaniment to Korean barbecue, in my opinion, along with *ssam* and *ssamjang*, this is especially excellent with Roasted Pork Belly (page 140). Mildly spicy and fruity *gochugaru* vinaigrette-dressed spring onions carry the sweet tartness of cider vinegar. I like to dress mine with a touch of sesame oil to impart a nutty aroma and silky mouthfeel. Spring onions should be sliced into thin strips. Do this by cutting them into 5cm (2in) batons first, then vertically slice each baton into thin strips. Do soak the sliced spring onions in cold water to remove any harshness – an ice-cold water bath is preferred to revive the onions. This will also wash off any slimy mucus in the green parts.

Makes enough for about 4 servings
1 big bunch of spring onions (scallions)

For the *gochugaru* vinaigrette
2 tbsp cider vinegar
1½ tbsp *gochugaru* (Korean red pepper flakes)
1 tbsp golden granulated sugar
1 tbsp soy sauce
1 tbsp toasted sesame oil
1 tsp toasted white sesame seeds

Mix together all the ingredients for the vinaigrette then gently toss in the spring onions. Do this when you're ready to serve, as the spring onions will wilt quickly if dressed in advance.

LA Short Ribs

I honestly can't think of any better dish to show off the flavour of Korean barbecue than these caramelized sugar-scented beef short ribs. More traditionally, individual sections of short ribs are butterflied and lengthened with the bone still attached at the end. The meat is then cleverly scored diagonally to allow the marinade to penetrate, tenderizing and flavouring an otherwise tougher cut. It is said that early Korean immigrants in Los Angeles had to adapt to cuts available in neighbourhood butchers, which sold more affordably priced flanken-cut short ribs used by Mexican immigrants, to recreate the flavours of distant home and invented the lateral-cut galbi, which is now widely recognized as LA Galbi. Flanken-style short ribs, also known in the UK as Korean-style short ribs, are readily available from many butchers and online.

The perfectly balanced, salty-sweet marinade lends finger-licking deliciousness that is truly hard to resist. Pre-marinating the meat with sugar and fruit helps not only to tenderize the meat but also enhances the sweetness, as sugar generally takes longer to fully penetrate the flesh than soy sauce. In the absence of Asian pear, replace it with another sweet variety of pear or half a kiwi.

This does need to marinate overnight if you are to properly enjoy the flavours; it is also best to cook it on a charcoal grill to maximize the smoky flavour.

Serves 4–6

1kg (2lb 4oz) lateral short-cut/Korean-style short ribs, fat trimmed

For the marinade
6 tbsp soft dark brown sugar
½ onion, roughly chopped
½ Asian pear, peeled, cored and roughly chopped
3 tbsp sake
3 tbsp mirin
6 tbsp soy sauce
3 tbsp water
3 tbsp toasted sesame oil
35g (1¼oz) garlic cloves, minced
3 spring onions (scallions), finely minced
1 tsp freshly cracked black pepper

Laterally cut short ribs sometimes have tiny particles of bone dust around the bones. If you notice it, briefly rinse the meat under running water, paying attention around the bones, to remove any dust. Pat the meat dry with kitchen paper to remove excess moisture if rinsed, or any sitting blood.

Transfer the meat to a container, layering with the sugar as you go (use all the sugar). Purée the onion, pear, sake and mirin in a food processor until smooth, then pour over the short ribs. Massage well to combine, then set aside for 10 minutes.

Mix the rest of the ingredients in a bowl and stir well to combine. Pour this over the short ribs and massage them again by hand to evenly coat the meat. Arrange the meat nice and flat, neatly stacked up. Cover and refrigerate for at least 4 hours or preferably overnight.

If cooking on an outdoor charcoal barbecue grill, cook the marinated ribs on the hot grill when the layer of white ash is visible over the glowing embers. It should take about 3–4 minutes to cook on each side until lightly charred and caramelized.

You can also cook the marinated ribs indoors in a heavy-based frying pan (skillet) or griddle pan. Heat the pan until nice and hot. Add the ribs to the pan in a single layer and immediately reduce the heat to medium. Cook for 4–5 minutes on one side, then turn to cook for a further 2–3 minutes. You may want to add a splash of water or a couple of spoonfuls of marinade if the frying pan appears too dry.

Alternatively, cook them under a hot oven grill (broiler).

Once cooked, cut the ribs into single sections or simply cut the meat off the bones into bite-size pieces. Serve immediately with a side of seasonal leaves and *Ssam* Sauce (page 222).

NOTES ON FRUIT PURÉE

-

The fruit and vegetable fibre present in puréed pulp is believed to encourage the marinade to burn more easily. Passing the puréed pear and onion through a muslin or cheesecloth to extract the liquid from the solid is quite commonly practised in Korean homes to prevent the meat from burning. If you wish to do so, set a fine sieve over the bowl and lay a muslin or cheesecloth over the sieve. Carefully pour the puréed mixture into the cloth-lined sieve. Secure the cloth tightly from the top so you can start wringing to push out the liquid into the bowl. Squeeze as hard you can to extract as much liquid as possible, pressing on the solids. Once all the liquid is collected, discard the pulp.

Doenjang Lamb Skewers

Lamb hasn't always been consumed widely, nor been readily available in Korea up until recent years. Most of those who tried lamb (it was thought to be mutton, actually) weren't so sure about the rich, almost pastoral taste and smell they recognized as gamey. But the steady increase of imported meat, and the introduction of cumin-spiced lamb skewers by Korean Chinese immigrants that sat more comfortably with the modern Korean palate, have greatly contributed to the increasing popularity of lamb, so people have become more familiar with the product and how best to cook with it.

This dish is inspired by the daring new flavour combinations created by the migration of people and ingredients, which are accepted and celebrated with love. The complexity of fermented bean paste pairs incredibly well with earthy lamb, taking the roll of 'spicing'. Laced with a tart sweetness that comes from the pomegranate molasses, this wildly unimaginable marriage of flavours actually creates a magic that I think is absolutely delicious.

Use a needle-bladed meat tenderizer so the marinade can properly penetrate into the flesh of the meat below the surface, and massage the meat by hand to work the marinade until it is fully absorbed. The skewers definitely benefit from being cooked on a charcoal grill: the smoky flavour that comes from slowly caramelized lamb is truly wonderful.

Makes 12 skewers

4 lamb neck fillets,
    about 650g–750g
    (1lb 7oz–1lb 10oz)
sea salt flakes, to season

For the marinade
15g (½oz) garlic cloves,
    minced
2 tsp grated ginger root
2 tbsp soft dark brown
    sugar
2 tbsp extra virgin olive oil
2 tbsp *doenjang* (Korean
    fermented bean paste)
2 tbsp pomegranate
    molasses
1 tbsp soy sauce
1 tbsp cider vinegar
1 tsp freshly cracked
    black pepper

Combine all the ingredients for the marinade in a large mixing bowl.

Slice the lamb neck fillets in half lengthways, then dice into 2cm (¾in) thick bite-size pieces suitable for your choice of skewers, bearing in mind they'll shrink a little when cooked.

Using a needle-bladed meat tenderizer, go over the diced lamb so the needles penetrate into the meat: it will help the marinade to permeate the tissue more deeply. Transfer the meat to the bowl of marinade and vigorously massage everything together to properly work the marinade into the meat. When the meat appears to have absorbed the marinade, cover and refrigerate for 4 hours or up to overnight.

Thread the marinated lamb onto the skewers (about 5 cubes each), making sure they are fairly tightly secured and flattened gently by hand as you

go along to ensure an even cooking surface. Repeat the process until you have about 12 skewers.

If cooking on an outdoor charcoal barbecue grill, cook the skewers on the hot grill when the layer of white ash is visible over the glowing embers. I like to give them a quarter turn every so often to char them evenly. It should take about 6 minutes for the lamb to cook through and appear beautifully charred and caramelized.

If you are cooking the skewers indoors, heat a griddle pan nice and hot over a medium heat. Place the skewers onto the hot griddle and cook for 3 minutes on each side until nicely caramelized. Alternatively, cook them under the oven grill (broiler).

When the skewers are done, sprinkle with a little pinch of sea salt flakes and serve immediately.

ON THE GRILL

Grilled Meat Patties

The story goes that this was originally a luxury dish enjoyed by kings in the royal court. Developed for the royals who were reluctant to pick up ribs with their hands, beautifully tender and rich meat was picked from the beef ribs then minced to form a patty before being put back on the thick rib bones, so the delicious flavour of charcoal-grilled ribs could still be enjoyed by the aristocracy. Since then, the dish has evolved through generations, and regional variations take many different shapes, with some favouring more accessibly priced minced meat.

I use half beef and half pork here to increase the chance of juiciness; pork also adds more flavour. These incredibly versatile patties can be used to fill soft buns to make a change from standard burgers, or served as part of a *ssam* spread, to be enjoyed wrapped in soft leaves with pickles and dips.

The patties really benefit from being cooked on a charcoal grill, as when the juices from the marinade drip onto the hot coals, a wonderful smoke will grace the meat. Though they'll still taste great if you cook them in a hot pan or under the grill (broiler).

In the recipe, I suggest you shape the meat to form patties but, to be honest, it is also perfectly fine to slap it onto a hot pan as one giant slab of deliciousness – whatever works best for you.

Place the pear, garlic and ginger in a food processor and blend to a smooth purée. Transfer to a large mixing bowl. Add the beef and pork to the bowl, along with the rest of the ingredients for the patties (except the vegetable oil). Start mixing everything together by hand to build up the strength and stickiness, energetically working the mixture as if you are kneading a dough. As you continue to work, the mixture will become paler with speckles of very fine white threads, then you are done.

Shape the mixture into 10 equal-sized square patties, about 1cm (½in) thick with rounded corners. Transfer them to a baking tray lined with parchment paper, cover and refrigerate for at least 1 hour and up to overnight, so the patties can firm up and soak up the flavour of the marinade.

Meanwhile, combine everything together for the finishing glaze and set aside.

To cook the patties on an outdoor charcoal barbecue, use a grilling basket with handles so you can easily flip them frequently. Cook the patties over a hot grill when the layer of white ash is visible over the glowing embers. They should take about 3–4 minutes to cook on each side.

If you are cooking indoors, heat some vegetable oil in a heavy-based frying pan (skillet) over a medium heat and cook the patties for 3–4 minutes on each side until cooked through.

When the patties are done, brush with the finishing glaze. Serve warm with a garnish of white sesame seeds and snipped chives.

Makes about 10 × 80g (3oz) patties

For the patties
¼ Asian pear, peeled, cored and roughly chopped
3 garlic cloves, crushed
1 tsp grated ginger root
300g (10½oz) minced (ground) beef
300g (10½oz) minced (ground) pork
3 tbsp soy sauce
2 tbsp soft light brown sugar
1 tbsp mirin
1 tbsp toasted sesame oil
1 tbsp toasted white sesame seeds
4 spring onions (scallions), finely minced
½ tsp freshly cracked black pepper
2 tbsp glutinous rice flour
vegetable oil, for frying, if you are cooking in a frying pan (skillet)

For the finishing glaze
1 tbsp toasted sesame oil
1 tsp honey
¼ tsp sea salt flakes

To serve
toasted white sesame seeds
snipped chives

Chicken Skewers with Sesame Chicken Skin Crumbs

Chicken skewers have long been one of the most popular Korean street foods. Perfectly bite-sized strips of dark meat (usually leg meat) are grilled over charcoal, then brushed with a lick of sauce, the recipe for which is the owners' well-kept secret. Chefs get quite theatrical blow-torching the top of the skewers while the undersides grill slowly over the charcoal heat to create what literally translates as 'fire taste' (*bul mat*).

The glaze I use here isn't spicy, rather it is balanced with sweet and umami saltiness that eats pleasantly. If you want to get ahead, it can be made in advance and will keep for a few days in the fridge. Crispy chicken skin crumbs make exceptionally good seasoning salt; the trouble is, they are actually just as good straight from the oven, which makes it hard to resist nibbling on them while waiting for the skewers to cook.

Curried Pot Rice (page 172) goes really well with this if you want to make it more of a meal, as does Beetroot-Stained Pickled Radish (page 90).

Serves 6 (makes about 12 skewers)

8 boneless chicken thighs, about 900g (2lb), skin left on
30g (1oz) ginger root
4 tbsp full-fat milk
2 tbsp sake
2 tbsp vegetable oil
1 tsp sea salt flakes
¼ tsp freshly cracked black pepper
12 spring onions (scallions), sliced into 3cm (1¼in) long batons
fine sea salt, to season

For the glaze

2 tbsp soft dark brown sugar
2 tbsp soy sauce
1 tbsp tomato ketchup (catsup)
1 tbsp *gochujang* (Korean red chilli paste)
100ml (3½fl oz/scant ½ cup) water
1 whole dried red chilli

For the chicken skin crumbs

1 tsp toasted white sesame seeds
¼ tsp sea salt flakes

To prepare the chicken, first remove the skin from the meat. Scrape off any excess fat from the underside of the skin and lay it stretched out flat in a baking tray lined with parchment paper. Sprinkle with a pinch of salt and refrigerate until needed.

Cut the skinless thighs into bite-sized cubes or strips suitable for your choice of skewers, bearing in mind they'll shrink a little when cooked, and transfer them to a large mixing bowl. Finely grate the ginger and squeeze out the pulp over the meat, so only the juice is collected in the bowl underneath. Discard the pulp. Add the milk, sake, vegetable oil, sea salt and black pepper. Massage everything together to combine. Cover and refrigerate to marinate for 4 hours or up to overnight.

If you are using wooden skewers, soak them in cold water for 30 minutes.

Meanwhile, whisk together all the ingredients for the glaze, except the dried red chilli, in a small saucepan. Once everything is well combined, add the chilli and simmer gently for 10 minutes until the sauce has thickened to the consistency of clear honey.

Preheat a fan oven to 180°C (350°F/gas 6).

Lightly grind the sesame seeds in a pestle and mortar. Stir in the flaked sea salt and transfer it to a small mixing bowl.

Put the tray of chicken skins in the oven and cook for 30 minutes until gorgeously crispy and puffed up in places. Transfer to a plate lined with kitchen paper to absorb any excess fat. When cooled down enough to handle, chop into crumbs and stir into the ground sesame and salt mixture. Set aside.

Thread the marinated chicken pieces onto the skewers, alternating 2 to 3 pieces of meat and a piece of spring onion. I like to thread them fairly tightly but flattened gently by hand as I go along, to ensure an even cooking surface. Repeat the process until you have about 12 skewers.

If you are cooking on an outdoor charcoal barbecue grill, cook the skewers on the hot grill when the layer of white ash is visible over glowing embers. I like to give them a quarter turn every so often to char them evenly. It should take about 6–8 minutes for the chicken to cook through and appear lightly charred and caramelized. Brush them with the glaze and let the sugar bubble and caramelize briefly before removing from the heat.

If you are cooking the skewers indoors, heat a griddle pan nice and hot over a medium heat. Place the skewers onto the hot griddle and cook for 3 minutes on the first side, then turn to cook for a further 4–5 minutes until all sides are nicely caramelized. Brush them with the glaze and let the sugar bubble and caramelize briefly before removing from the heat.

Alternatively, cook them under the oven grill (broiler).

To serve, you can either sprinkle the chicken skin crumbs liberally on top of the skewers or serve it as a dipping salt on the side. Enjoy while warm.

Korean Fried Chicken

It is quite likely that I'm chasing perfection that doesn't really exist. In my vivid dreams, this fried chicken tastes intently sweet but not sickly. Deep nutty background sweetness lingers like an intense pull of stupid first love that you fail to resist, and is only accentuated by the heat of chilli and umami salinity that hugs the fat. It's not claggy – smothered in thick paste of *gochujang* – but rather softly candied like a buttery caramel-coated popcorn.

I am unsure if such a glorious perfection of taste can be replicated. But I keep going back for more, no longer sure if I am craving the chicken or my home so many miles away.

Dak means 'chicken'. And the name *gangjeong* derives from the type of traditional Korean confection of that name, made by steaming fermented rice flour dough, then deep-frying it until puffed before glazing it in honey or the traditional rice syrup, *jocheong,* and coating in ground seeds or nuts. *Dakgangjeong* is made in a similar way, by glazing the fried chicken pieces in syrup-heavy sauce to generously coat the crackly crust and give the dish unmistakable viscosity and shine.

Rice syrup has a softer sweetness than sugar, and a faint butterscotch taste with umami undertones. In the absence of rice syrup, a simple mixture of sugar dissolved in hot water in equal ratio, with a touch of maple syrup to flavour, can make a reasonable substitution. But I do think it is worth trying the recipe with rice syrup, as the substitution will give the dish a different finish (it sets differently). After all, it wouldn't be a *gangjeong* without the dominant appearance of traditional syrup, which can easily be found in Korean supermarkets or online.

Serves 4

For the chicken
600g (1lb 5oz) boneless, skinless chicken thighs, cut into 3cm (1¼in) cubes
2 tbsp sake
1 tsp golden granulated sugar
½ tsp celery salt
½ tsp freshly cracked black pepper
vegetable oil, for frying

For the glaze
60g (2oz) *jocheong* (Korean rice syrup)
2 tbsp tomato ketchup (catsup)
2 tbsp water
1 tbsp golden granulated sugar
1 tbsp soy sauce
1 tbsp *gochujang* (Korean red chilli paste)
3 garlic cloves, minced
1 tbsp vegetable oil
1 tbsp *gochugaru* (Korean red pepper flakes), ground to a fine powder

For the batter
50g (1¾oz/heaped ⅓ cup) plain (all-purpose) flour
70g (2½oz/½ cup) rice flour
20g (¾oz/scant ¼ cup) cornflour (cornstarch)
150ml (5fl oz/scant ⅔ cup) cold water

To finish
toasted white sesame seeds

Place the chicken pieces in a mixing bowl, along with the sake, sugar, celery salt and black pepper. Massage well to combine, cover and leave to marinate in the fridge for 1 hour.

To make the glaze, combine the *jocheong*, ketchup, water, sugar, soy sauce, *gochujang* and garlic in a bowl. Mix well and set aside.

Remove the chicken from the fridge so it comes back to room temperature before you cook it.

Put the vegetable oil and *gochugaru* in a cold wok or sauté pan over a low heat to warm up, stirring constantly to prevent the *gochugaru* from burning – a flat flexible spatula is great for this. In a few minutes, the oil will change in colour to a deep red and the *gochugaru* will start to bloom. Swiftly add the glaze mixture and increase the heat to rapidly bubble for about 2 minutes to thicken the sauce enough to coat the back of the spoon like a runny custard, but not yet sticky like wet glue. Remove from the heat and set aside.

Prepare the wet batter by combining the plain flour, 30g (1oz) of the rice flour and the cornflour. Add the water gradually to the mix and whisk to break up any lumps.

→

Meat

Toss the chicken thoroughly with the remaining 40g (1½oz) rice flour then add the chicken to the batter. Give it a good mix by hand.

Prepare a cooling rack set over a roasting tray.

To fry the chicken, fill a saucepan suitable for deep-frying with vegetable oil. It should be deep enough to submerge the chicken pieces but only come three-quarters of the way up the pan while you are frying. Heat the oil to 160°C (320°F). Carefully lower in a few of the battered chicken pieces and fry for 2–3 minutes until the chicken is cooked through but only pale golden, transferring them onto the cooling rack when they're done to allow the steam to escape. Don't put too many in at once. Continue until you have cooked all the chicken. This first fry is to cook the chicken through, so it shouldn't have too much colour. Check for doneness.

Once the first fry is done, increase the heat to 175°C (347°F) and fry for the second time for 2–3 minutes until they're golden and crispy. Work in batches to prevent overcrowding the pan. When the batches are ready, transfer them onto the cooling rack so any excess oil drains off. Don't be tempted to sit the chicken on kitchen paper as it will just steam and lose its crispiness.

Put the wok or sauté pan with the sauce over a medium heat to warm up. As soon as the edges start to bubble up, toss in the fried chicken while energetically moving the pan around to glaze. In a brief moment, the sauce will coat the chicken and thicken around the crusts. Remove from the heat and sprinkle with sesame seeds. Serve immediately with Beetroot-Stained Pickled Radish (page 90).

ON THE HOB, IN THE OVEN + RAW

Poached Pork Belly Wrap

My mother's kitchen was never short of good boiled pork, usually cooked with a handsome bit of shoulder or leg with a little fat and always without the skin. It was always eaten on the day we batched kimchi, to feast together with those who came to lend a hand, generously sliced and served with the tender inner leaves of salted cabbage. We ate it with *kimchi-so* (kimchi fillings) smothered with *gochugaru* paste and studded with freshly shucked winter oysters.

My mother's braising liquor was dark and perfumed with cinnamon bark, and the meat tasted as though it had been bathed in fermented bean paste soup. Perfectly crunchy and spicy fillings complemented the tender pork wonderfully, resulting in bold yet balanced flavours that were wrapped in soft cabbage leaves with layers of heat and roundness bleeding out to burst in the mouth.

Bossam to me is a dish that symbolizes the culture of community and reunion, and the taste of my mother's loving hand that brought people closer together at the table.

I daringly use the pork belly with the skin deliberately left on. As the pork gently poaches in the cooking liquid, fat renders slowly to yield moist flesh, and the skin becomes exquisitely gelatinous. If you are unsure about the soft skin, simply remove it before cooking.

I recommend you try the dish with simple blanched white cabbage and *Ssamjang* Sauce (page 222) on the side to bolster the wrap together; the sweet taste of cabbage really complements the fatty pork and carries the strength of *ssamjang* really well. Otherwise, serve with pliable seasonal leaves that are suitable for wrapping.

Serves 6

2 tbsp soft dark brown sugar
3 tbsp blackstrap molasses
3 tbsp sake
3 tbsp soy sauce
1 tbsp *doenjang* (Korean fermented bean paste)
1 litre (34fl oz/4 cups) water
1 tbsp black peppercorns
½ onion, skin left on
½ apple, cored with skin left on
100g (3½oz) leek, halved lengthways
40g (1½oz) garlic cloves, lightly crushed
15g (½oz) ginger root, roughly sliced
2 dried bay leaves
1kg (2lb 4oz) pork belly, cut into 5cm (2in) wide strips with skin left on
1 cinnamon stick

Serve with blanched white cabbage or seasonal leaves for wrapping and *Ssamjang* sauce (page 222).

Whisk together the sugar, blackstrap molasses, sake, soy sauce, *doenjang* and water in a heavy-based saucepan or stockpot with a lid. Add all the remaining ingredients except the pork belly and cinnamon stick. Bring to the boil, then simmer for 15 minutes over a medium heat with the lid left on ajar.

Carefully submerge the pork belly into the poaching liquid and add the cinnamon stick. Reduce the heat immediately. Simmer very gently for 1¼ hours until the meat is cooked through but not completely falling apart. Turn the heat off and let the pork rest in the pan for at least 15 minutes.

Remove the pork from the pan and ensure the meat has cooled down enough to touch. Discard the poaching liquid. Slice the meat into 5mm (¼in) thick slices, then transfer it to a large platter.

If you are planning on serving later, cover the meat before slicing and refrigerate until needed. When ready to serve, slice as above, then steam for a few minutes to reheat.

Serve the sliced pork with your choice of pliable seasonal leaves to wrap, with *Ssamjang* Sauce (page 222) on the side. Spicy Radish Salad (page 36) also makes a great accompaniment.

Roasted Pork Belly

I adore roast pork belly. It's the dish that brings me sweet memories of my emerging adulthood, when nights were beautifully young and free and I crawled the narrow streets of university towns, chock full of neighbourhood barbecue restaurants, looking for cheap *soju* and crispy slices of pork belly.

This is barely a recipe but I wanted to share my love for well-roasted pork belly that I feel eats the closest to tabletop grills back in the neon-light-filled streets of Seoul. A toothsomely sliced slab of perfectly three-layered meat flaunting the buttery melt-in-your-mouth fat that renders slowly to yield beautifully fork tender meat nuanced with the complex salinity of *doenjang*, and superbly crispy crackling that you will be proud of. Serve with a full spread of *ssam*, a bouquet of soft seasonal leaves and herbs for wrapping, sesame oil and salt dipping sauce, Spring Onion Salad (page 125) and *ssamjang* (page 222). And believe in that pork-fat glow!

Serves 4

1kg (2lb 4oz) pork belly, bones removed
1 tbsp sake
1 tbsp *doenjang* (Korean fermented bean paste)
sea salt flakes, to season

Pat the pork dry, paying attention to the skin to ensure it is free of moisture. The skin does not need to be scored.

Combine the sake and *doenjang* in a small mixing bowl. Brush the runny paste onto all meat sides of the belly, leaving the skin completely untouched. Refrigerate the meat, skin-side up and uncovered, for at least 24 hours or preferably two days, so the meat can brine and the skin can dry out completely.

Preheat a fan oven to 150°C (300°F/ gas 3–4).

Remove the meat from the fridge 30 minutes before cooking so it is not fridge cold. Carefully wipe off the *doenjang* and sake paste with kitchen paper. Place the pork onto a large sheet of foil, meat-side down, and start folding four edges to protect the exposed flesh of the pork, leaving the skin uncovered. You want to wrap it as tightly as possible as the meat will shrink a little as it cooks. Transfer the meat to a roasting tin and sprinkle the skin with a little salt. Roast the pork in the middle of the oven for 2 hours.

Remove the pork from the oven and increase the temperature to 220°C (425°F/gas 8).

Meanwhile carefully pour out the rendered fat into a heatproof jar; once cooled down, you can store the fat in the fridge and use it for cooking. Keep the pork flesh protected with foil, with the skin still uncovered. Once the oven reaches the desired temperature, put the pork back in and roast for 20 minutes to crisp up the skin. Once done, remove from the oven. Transfer it to a plate or chopping board and rest the meat for 30 minutes before slicing.

To serve, slice the meat into bite-size pieces. It is best to cut skin-side down with a sharp knife. Transfer the meat to a large platter and serve with all the trimmings mentioned above.

Raw Beef Salad

This is a plate of beautifully messy raw beef, dressed simply in a traditional way with a little honey and salt, laced with fragrant toasted sesame oil. The dish reminds me of family dinners at my auntie's house and her delicate hands – how tiny, pale and fragile they sometimes looked, but also how those fingertips moved fiercely across the kitchen like a dancer's feet.

It used to be my father's favourite thing to eat at my auntie's house, as my mother seldom made *yukhoe* at home. Paired with refreshingly juicy sweet pear, fine ribbons of soft beef turn just the right side of sweet and deliciously savoury, with raw egg yolk cracked on top to show off the crimson red flesh of the beef. A generous quantity of freshly cracked black pepper is the key, I think, to emphasize the true taste of beef. As with any simple food pairing, there isn't much to hide behind here, so you will need to get the best and freshest piece of beef.

Seasoned, toasted seaweed sheets make a nice accompaniment to wrap the beef; its umami notes carry beef really well.

Serves 2–4

350g (12oz) beef bavette

For the seasoning
1 tsp golden granulated sugar
1 garlic clove, finely minced
2 spring onions (scallions), white parts only, finely minced
2 tbsp toasted sesame oil
1 tbsp clear honey
1 tsp soy sauce
1 tsp freshly cracked black pepper
1 tsp toasted sesame seeds, lightly crushed
1 tsp sea salt flakes, to season

To finish
½ Asian pear
2–4 egg yolks (optional)
toasted black sesame seeds, to garnish
roasted seaweed sheets, to serve

Pat the beef dry with kitchen paper to remove any sitting blood. Slice as thinly as possible against the grain, then again to cut into fine strips, if necessary. Transfer to a large mixing bowl.

Sprinkle the sugar on top of the beef and add the rest of the seasoning ingredients. Toss everything together to thoroughly coat the beef with seasoning, as quickly as you can with a gentle touch of your fingertips. You don't want to overwork the meat. Once combined, check for seasoning and adjust with a pinch more salt if necessary. Place a sheet of clingfilm (plastic wrap) directly over, so there is no gap between the meat and the clingfilm. Then cover and store it in the fridge for 1 hour to chill.

When ready to serve, peel and core the pear, then julienne it into matchsticks. Divide the cold marinated beef between plates. Place the egg yolks in the middle, if using. Scatter the pear around and finish with a sprinkle of black sesame seeds on top. Serve immediately with roasted seaweed sheets.

This also makes a great topping for *Bibimbap* (page 166).

Meat   143

Fish

five

it was all pure + simple love

My father used to own a small record player. The old vinyls he played always crackled over his softly humming voice that was often slightly off key. But it wasn't difficult to notice the sense of appreciation in his voice for the sound that he found soothing.

He was the kind of father who took us fishing in the lakes in summer when the weekend was forecast sunny, slinging an impromptu picnic bag and a tent on his shoulder. He dragged all of us on the train heading south in the middle of the night and made us climb up thousands of stairs to show us the roaring sunrise above and across the tranquil blue ocean.

He woke us up on Sunday mornings with a blast of the song 'Bridge Over Troubled Water', and comically demanded the 'all rise' in a militant north Korean accent that made us crack up in tears. Even he thought it was funny and could barely keep a straight face.

We went to the Noryangjin fish market at least once a month when the soft-lipped early morning breeze gently kissed our fingertips as we stroked the moving wind from the back of the car. Our limbs were curled up softly into balls while our unruly hair freely waved away the passing cars.

The river we followed shined with glistening light to twinkle the 63 Building across the market; the tall flashy golden building glowed as if our dreams were made of gold. Life felt magical in that light.

My father knew where to go for what fish and always gave us the grand tour of the market. He had a name for every moving thing in each water tank or bucket, and always had a place for it in the kitchen. He bought live crabs to make into a stew for dinner and made us try perfectly sliced raw flesh of fish dipped in vinegar-laced *gochujang* paste before we knew it was *hoe* – a Korean word for sashimi.

As chaotic as their lives were as young working parents, they built a routine around the stable rhythms that made our ordinary family life feel safe and happy. We went to the movies on Saturdays and ate dinners at restaurants famous for the next trendy thing, and spent rainy Sundays rolling sheets of noodles together while listening to my father reminisce about his upbringing as a child of the post-war era. He woke us up early in the mornings, making fun of himself to make us laugh, and tried to show us the whole wide world beyond the four small walls of our house, where our dreams could be made into sweet shades of candy floss if we wanted.

I remember him singing the Frank Sinatra song 'My Way' in the car on our way home. He sang in the same playful way he used to hum Simon and Garfunkel but with a self-assured conviction that felt like a nod to his beliefs and values. There was a sense of pride that carried in his voice as a father who was able to provide in relative ease, away from all that poverty and hunger that used to suck the life out of his soul.

Not long after I had my daughter, I listened to the lyrics of the songs he used to listen to; I sat in silence vacantly glaring at the distance with the wisps of my voice whimpering the words that used to mean nothing much more than our trips to the fish market and his smiley, tired, round face.

I felt the words etched into the small bones I carry beneath my heart and wondered if he might have felt lonely at times, like I do sometimes, wondered if he ever felt loved.

He used to tell us how he had to choose the path of hard labouring work despite his desire to learn and succeed academically. And that he tried to live the dutiful life as the eldest of four, with heavy responsibilities from a very young age, to support his desperately poor family.

I thought of his happily drunk, clumsy hands that fed me square-shaped ice-cream wrapped in posh silver-foil paper in the middle of night – which used to be one of my favourite things in the whole world – and felt his *soju*-breathed chin that used to rub my cheeks scratchily. I wondered if he'd suffered quietly, burying all the desires somewhere deep to stop them seeping out and bleeding red raw again. He forged forward only to succeed in the path he'd chosen, to become the kind of good father and husband that his own father couldn't be. I can see now just how hard he worked not to repeat history; not to be that parent.

I sat in silence for a while, gasping for some air to steady my shaky heart that was weeping for my father for the first time. It took me to have my own child to see that he shared his shy heart in his own funny kind of ways, and I know now that it was all love, pure and simple.

Fried Flat Fish with *Yangnyeom* Dressing

I think the simple cooking of fish is often overlooked when it comes to the rising fame of Korean food in the West. While the ever-growing popularity of teeth-shatteringly crispy Korean fried chicken or the beautiful mess of technicolored vegetable-topped *bibimbap* continues to grab the attention of many, dishes like this have sadly missed opportunities to be properly introduced, which is such a pity.

Cooking fish here is incredibly simple: pan-fried, seasoned with plenty of salt, and dusted with flour to create a thin crust. Magic happens when you drench the top of golden, crispy fish skin with the heavenly soy sauce dressing that tastes complex yet delicate enough to coherently bind the sweet flesh of flat fish. You can just about notice the subtle cumin-like perfume of perilla oil carrying the soft acidity of rice vinegar, which brings everything together into something gloriously salty, sweet and tangy. I think it's pure class.

I like to fry the whole flat fish but you can use fillets instead if that is more convenient: the same method of cooking can be applied, albeit with an adjusted cooking time to suit the thickness of the fish. The only thing to be mindful of is the size of the whole fish as it can often be too big to fit in an ordinary domestic frying pan (skillet). In which case, you would want to portion the fish into more manageable sizes.

Serves 2–4 depending on the size of the fish

1 whole flat fish, weighing about 600g (1lb 5oz) (brill, plaice, sole, flounder or skate)
sea salt flakes, to season
plain (all-purpose) flour, for dusting
vegetable oil, for frying
2 tsp thin julienne matchsticks of ginger root

For the dressing
1 tbsp golden granulated sugar
1 tbsp soup or light soy sauce
1 tbsp perilla oil
1 tbsp rice vinegar
2 tbsp water
1 tsp wholegrain mustard
2 tbsp red onion, finely diced
1 spring onion (scallion), minced
1 mild red chilli, deseeded and sliced
½ tsp toasted white sesame seeds
¼ tsp freshly cracked black pepper

Combine all the ingredients for the dressing in a small bowl. Set aside.

Pat the fish dry with kitchen paper and season both sides with salt; be mindful of seasoning if you are using smaller fillets or portioned fish. Dust the fish generously with flour and shake off any excess.

Heat some vegetable oil in a very large frying pan (skillet) or smooth flat grill pan, ideally rimmed, so it can hold the frying oil. Keep the heat on medium. The oil shouldn't be screaming hot – just enough to hear the gentle sizzle when you add the fish to the pan. Fry the fish for 4–5 minutes on each side until the skin forms a crispy crust and turns beautifully golden.

Transfer to a platter and douse generously with the dressing. Scatter the ginger on top and serve immediately with a steaming bowl of plain rice on the side.

Grilled Salt + Sugar-Cured Mackerel

Mackerel in Korea is often sold pre-brined in heavily salted water, then salted again for preservation, swaddled tightly in coarse white mineral-rich crystals. Its delicate ocean blue skin becomes taught and its flesh turns firm and meaty. It smells like the sea and eats like the holiday barbecue of dreams with sandy feet treading in and out of the water, swigging cold beers with the waft of a charcoal-grilled catch of the day tickling your throat.

Properly salt-cured mackerel is treasured for its delicious flavour thanks to the magical bacterial transformation that happens during the curing process. It greatly improves the taste of the fish, intensifying every morsel of flesh and skin into a mouthwatering gift of the ocean.

The simple curing I use here is by no means an answer to the wonder of a heavy cure, but rather a user-friendly way to enjoy oily fish and replicate the flavours I grew up to adore. And I hope you will, too.

Grill gently over the embers of coals if weather permits, otherwise slide it under the oven grill (broiler) until the skin chars and blisters. Anise Pickled Rhubarb (page 92) is particularly good on the side, so is the Onion Salad with Wasabi Soy Vinaigrette (page 125). But equally, a squeeze of lemon is just fine, too.

Serves 2, or 4 as a starter

2 mackerel, heads removed, cleaned and butterflied, or 4 fillets
2 tsp sea salt flakes
2 tsp golden granulated sugar
1 tbsp sake
1 tbsp vegetable oil
lemon wedges, to serve

Pat the fish dry with kitchen paper and lay them on a flat tray in one single layer, skin-side down. Sprinkle evenly with half the salt and sugar, then turn to lay them skin-side up and sprinkle with the rest of the salt and sugar. Refrigerate uncovered for a minimum of 1 hour and up to overnight.

Preheat the oven grill (broiler) on high. Line a shallow-rimmed, grill-safe baking tray with foil and place it in the oven to heat. This is so when the fish is laid onto the hot tray, it starts to cook immediately from both top and bottom.

Combine the sake and vegetable oil in a bowl.

Remove the mackerel from the fridge and gently brush the sake and oil mixture on both sides of the fish. Carefully remove the foil-lined tray from the oven, which should be nice and hot. Place the mackerel skin-side up and grill on high for about 4 minutes until the skin chars and blisters in places. There is no need to flip to cook the flesh side – it should be perfectly cooked.

To serve, transfer to individual plates with wedges of lemon on the side.

Fish

Grilled Clams with Sweet *Doenjang* Vinaigrette

Despite the rising interest in Korean barbecues, cooking of shellfish on charcoal isn't practised or talked about much in the West when we share our enthusiasm for Korean grills.

Here, I have taken inspiration from many plates of grilled shellfish I enjoyed during my visit to Busan, a large coastal city known for its breathtakingly beautiful scenery, rich food culture and generous hospitality.

Shellfish kept in their own shells and cooked on the barbecue don't require much more than a fish grill basket to hold everything together if they're too small – even a makeshift foil tray with a few holes at the bottom will do the job. As the smouldering embers gently heat up to open the firmly closed shells, smoke rises to perfume the sweet flesh. It cooks to perfection in its own juice with hardly any effort. I am opting for the convenience of a domestic grill as more practical, although, weather permitting, you could grill them directly on the barbecue.

Try stirring through thin noodles or use a chewy baguette to mop up the sauce, which is far too good to waste.

Combine all the ingredients for the dressing in a bowl and set aside.

Preheat the oven grill (broiler) to high. Place a grill-safe baking tray in the oven to heat. This is so when the shellfish are laid onto the hot tray, they start to cook immediately from both top and bottom.

Carefully remove the tray from the oven, which should be nice and hot. Place the clams (and/or any other shellfish you have selected) onto the hot tray as evenly as possible. Grill on high until the shells open and the flesh is cooked through – it should take about 5–7 minutes. Discard any that remain closed.

Meanwhile char the lime halves on a hot griddle pan (if grilling on a barbecue, cook them directly on the grill).

To serve, transfer the shellfish to a large sharing platter. Strain the juices collected at the bottom of the grill pan through a fine sieve, then pour this over the shellfish. Pour the dressing over and squeeze the grilled lime halves over the top too.

Serves 2–4 as a shared platter

1kg (2lb 4oz) clams, cleaned and purged if necessary (try different types of clams, mussels or scallops)
1 lime, halved

For the dressing
4 tbsp water
2 tbsp cider vinegar
2 tbsp mirin
1½ tbsp *doenjang* (Korean fermented bean paste)
1 tbsp perilla oil
1 tbsp soy sauce
1 tsp golden granulated sugar
1 tsp *gochugaru* (Korean red pepper flakes)
½ tsp freshly cracked black pepper
⅓ mild long red chilli, finely chopped
2 garlic cloves, minced
1 tsp grated ginger root
2 spring onions (scallions), thinly sliced

Spicy Squid Salad

If your wilting appetite demands nothing but the fiery kick of chilli and bright sourness to perk things up, I think this is the dish that will swiftly make your mouth water.

The sauce here is punchy with lingering heat of smoky *gochujang* and fruity *gochugaru* which tapers into the vibrant vinegar-laced sweetness that pools at the sides of the cheeks.

There isn't much cooking involved; just a messy assembly of julienned vegetables and quickly blanched strips of squid brought together by hand to pinch and massage so you can tease out and mould the flavours in harmony. The gentle pressure you apply with your fingertips to toss the vegetables will soften them a touch, especially the cabbages, allowing the contrasting textures to sit comfortably amongst one another.

I score the inner side of the squid tube, once opened flat, so the cracks of scored flesh catch the sauce in a way smooth flesh can't; it also curls beautifully when cooked. Of course, it isn't a must and you can absolutely skip the scoring, but as with most simple dishes, I think it is the small details that really can help to improve the overall result.

Serves 4

For the sauce
2 tbsp golden granulated sugar
2 tbsp *gochugaru* (Korean chilli flakes)
2 tbsp soy sauce
1 tbsp perilla oil
1½ tbsp *gochujang* (Korean fermented chilli paste)
3 tbsp cider vinegar
3 garlic cloves, minced

For the squid
2 medium-sized squid, about 350g (12oz) cleaned weight), cleaned and skins removed (you can ask fishmongers do this for you)
1 tbsp cider vinegar
40g (1½oz) carrot, julienned
130g (4½oz) cucumber, halved and sliced diagonally
130g (4½oz) white cabbage, shredded, soaked in cold water for 10 minutes, then drained
¼ red onion, thinly sliced, soaked in cold water for 10 minutes, then drained
1 tbsp parsley leaves
sea salt flakes, to season

To finish
1 mild green chilli, sliced
toasted white sesame seeds

Combine all the ingredients for the sauce in a small mixing bowl. Cover and refrigerate until needed.

Open the tube of squid flat by inserting a sharp knife inside to cut along the natural line. Once flat, scrape off any membranes and rinse under running water. Pat the squid dry with kitchen paper. Score the inside of the body in a criss-cross pattern with a sharp knife, ensuring the knife is only inserted about one third of the way into the flesh. Slice into bite-size rectangular strips. Cut the tentacles into the same-length pieces. Repeat with the other squid.

To blanch the squid, bring a pan of salted water to the boil. Add the vinegar and wait for a moment to bring it back up to a rapid boil. It is useful to have a bowl of cold water ready, close by, so you can plunge the blanched squid immediately into the cold water. Cook the squid strips for 1 minute, then transfer to the bowl of cold water, then drain.

Place the carrot, cucumber, cabbage and onion into a large mixing bowl, along with the parsley leaves. Add the drained squid to the bowl. Pour in the sauce and massage the ingredients by hand to combine, gently pinching and squeezing to bring it together. Check for seasoning and add a pinch more salt, if you like.

To serve, transfer the squid to a platter or divide between two plates. Scatter the chilli and toasted sesame seeds on top. The salad is good on its own or can be served with thin wheat noodles on the side to be stirred through to make it a more substantial meal.

Fish

Soy Sauce Marinated Prawns

This is a treasured delicacy in Korea, especially during the cooler autumn months when the prawns in season become perfectly plump and sweet, and not too big.

Not dissimilar to the better-known raw marinated crab dish called *Ganjang Gyejang*, prawns are marinated in a soy sauce-based brine infused with a medley of aromatics until the flavours of the lightly piquant sauce permeate deep into the delicate flesh of the prawns. The salty-sweet brine boldly punctuating the umami salinity of soy sauce is just as praise-worthy as the prawns themselves. As the sauce liberally seasons a steaming bowl of pearly white rice, it leaves trails of salty-sweet deliciousness in your mouth.

The dish certainly lives up to champion its nickname 'rice thief' and effortlessly moves between the mouthful of beautifully salty, starchy heaven and tenderly cured sweet prawns.

The brine here is a really straightforward process: chuck it all in a pot and simmer. The only thing to remember is to reboil the same brine on day three to ensure the concentration of liquid, as the prawns will release some moisture while marinating.

The dish will keep fresh for up to seven days in the fridge or you can portion and freeze for later use, which you can defrost in the fridge the night before. Eat while they're relatively young, as left sitting in the brine for too long the prawns become too salty and the flavour will spoil.

Makes enough to fill a 2 litre (70fl oz/ 8 cup) sterilized container

1kg (2lb 4oz) fresh raw prawns (shrimp), medium sized

For the brine
400ml (13fl oz/generous 1½ cups) water
200ml (7fl oz/scant 1 cup) soy sauce
70ml (2½fl oz/scant ⅓ cup) mirin
70ml (2½fl oz/scant ⅓ cup) sake
70g (2½oz/heaped ⅓ cup) golden granulated sugar
30g (1oz) garlic cloves, lightly crushed
20g (¾oz) ginger root, roughly sliced
five 5 × 7.5cm (2 × 3in) sheets of *dasima* (dried kelp)
½ onion, roughly sliced
½ apple, peeled, cored and cut in large chunks
2 dried red chillies, left whole
1 tbsp black peppercorns
3cm (1¼in) cinnamon stick

To finish
½ lemon, sliced
½ onion, sliced
chopped chillies, to serve (optional)

To prepare the prawns, decide if you are going to marinate them whole or with the heads removed. If you are keeping the heads on, using a pair of kitchen scissors, snip off the pointy mouth ends and spiky spines on top of the head. If you are removing the heads, gently twist and pull away the heads from the bodies – collected prawn heads can be used for making stocks or fragrant prawn oil for later use.

Devein the prawns and snip off the sharp needle-like telson from the tails. Once trimmed, wash thoroughly under cold running water. Drain, cover and refrigerate until needed.

Combine all the ingredients for the brine in a small saucepan. Bring to a gentle boil and simmer for 25 minutes over a low heat, stirring occasionally to ensure the sugar has fully dissolved. Remove from the heat and cool completely before passing it through a fine sieve to strain. Discard the solids.

Arrange the cleaned prawns in a sterilized container with a lid. Scatter with the sliced onion and lemon, then pour the brine over to completely submerge the prawns. Place a sheet of clingfilm (plastic wrap) directly over the top so there is no gap between the prawns and the clingfilm. Then cover with a lid and store it in the fridge for two days without touching. On day three, carefully pour out the soy sauce brine into a saucepan and bring to the boil: refrigerate the prawns in the same container while processing the brine. Cool the reboiled brine completely before pouring it back over the prawns.

To serve, transfer the desired quantity of prawns onto individual serving plates or a platter. Spoon over a ladleful of marinade, along with some marinated onions. Scatter with chopped chillies, if you like, then serve immediately with plain steamed rice to smoosh into the cold sauce.

Fish

Rice

six

a family who eats together stays together

My sister once sent me letter. The sister who was always good and obedient; the one who never crossed the line. She stood in to fill the gaps when I left home to free my suffocating brain on the other side of the ocean. My little sister became the eldest and stayed closer to my parents.

She saw my mother sigh over dinner many nights in a row. She was the one who had to pick up the pieces when my parents quibbled about unpaid bills mounting up. Things back home tasted sour and bitter even from a distance. Phone calls with my mother became less frequent but lengthy. There was a certain kind of tone that screamed anger and despair. I dreaded her calls, and the way she blamed everyone for every small thing drowned me.

Apparently, my parents argued day and night. My mother tried to salvage the pieces of her broken life from the wreckage while my father stood stubbornly, believing some kind of miracle would save them. He'd worked hard through the rain and snow, to turn the dust into pennies. Such loss of his fortune overnight did not register in his head. The hunger-driven blood that ran deep in his veins refused to accept the truth until the men in uniforms came to put stickers on everything my family owned. They emptied out my vacant bedroom full of nostalgia and took away my old piano. Things happened slowly but also cruelly fast. It took them a lifetime to build a life that felt comfortable at last, but it all vanished into thin air as though it was all just a dream. My mother wept in silence and my father did not know where and how to start all over again.

It didn't seem fair. But it was all gone. Part of who I am, also felt lost.

My mother did not struggle where she was left, nor was she frightened of her future. Though, this is only what I assumed; not fully the truth.

The blurry lines in the letter from my sister told of where my parents had moved to and the other in-between things I ought to know. I sat on the floor, not knowing what to feel. I just wanted to eat my mother's rice porridge, to scoop and swallow reluctantly while gazing into the far distance. Every word hit me like a brick and my heart felt black and blue. I was desperate to shake off the shivering air that kept clinging to my numbing skin. But I was left alone howling, not knowing where my home was now.

My sister signed her letter off with, 'Don't worry. And make sure to eat (rice).'

I know that was the day I lost a piece of me. I lost the only thing that gave me the illusion of the home I came from. There was no longer a home I could return to. Anything and everything that used to belong to me to remind me of my youth, teenage years, childhood, the beginning, no longer existed in ways I could feel or touch. It was only left in my head to reimagine and dream to fill the gaps.

My mother told me to hold it together. 'You lost a home, not a mother,' was what she would often say to stop me from shedding tears of sadness. It got stuck in my throat like a big lump of stone that I could neither swallow nor throw up. It took me years to realize how paralysed I was then. And just how hungry I was for the sense of home.

She once or twice said, 'Is it because I threw away the money carelessly?' It could be true. I sometimes wondered that too. One summer when my mother was angry with my father, she threw away her handbag full of cash. The night was terribly humid with torrential rain. The entire week's – or even month's – takings were mostly left on the side of a wet road, where the water channelled into the gutter. She returned home, with my father carrying the bag of wet cash. He left again for fresh air, or might have stormed off to the bedroom.

Both of my siblings and I listened to my mother sit in silence, not knowing how to fix the situation. Three of us unpacked the tightly stuck sodden notes and lay them

out onto the heated floor to dry out. When my mother was finished with her empty stare, she casually murmured she didn't care about the money, and suggested we order some pizza and a giant bottle of Coca-Cola. She didn't bother with cooking. My father went without food, his appetite lost, while the rest of us all sat together to picnic on the floor with boxes of thick-crust pizza topped with sliced, salty, bitter black olives and cubed green and yellow peppers. My mother did not talk about what happened. Instead, she unwillingly chomped on dry crusts, joking about how some lucky person might land on the rest of the sodden cash. She ate her feelings while we swallowed the atmosphere.

Pizza is still not my favourite thing to eat, in the same way that I am frightened to eat brothy cold *naengmyeon* noodles as I once choked badly on them. Funny that it took me these many years to figure out why. Even the struggles I had after becoming a mother started to make more sense.

My mother used to say that I was always a difficult child. So much so, she was only able to stomach a few grains of raw rice in the early days in order to sustain her pregnancy with me. I know I challenged her values relentlessly. I persistently negotiated my beliefs against hers and my fathers. She often told me to wait until I had a child just like me and then see what it feels like to be a mother. But she was also the one who always told me to go and see the world and be whoever I wanted to be.

When my daughter was born, I missed my mother terribly, all

the while feeling relieved that she was not there to tell me what to do. I was angry at the thought of my mother's absence. I wanted her to make me bowls of steaming hot rice steeped in seaweed soup like any other Korean mum. I would have quite liked her to shush my baby to sleep in her arms, so I could recover from the cuts and sores of the birth. Instead, I stood up every evening to cook whatever I could manage, to feel some sense of control to reassure me that everything I ever needed was all here. Though, it didn't take long for me to crumble. And I did eventually let my fragile mind shatter into millions of pieces, to let it all run wild. A small part of me knew I had to find my own way home to myself, to be the mother that I wanted to be.

When my mother spent a couple of summers in Florence, in an act of exercising her long-forgotten freedom, we finally met up in the foreign city. My pink and olive-skinned daughter with dark brown hair saw my mother for the first time. She was already almost two and a half years old and spoke good English for her age, but barely knew any Korean words other than *umma* or *appa*. My mother wanted to hold her granddaughter tight, but my baby held my fingers tighter, unsure of the strange faced woman speaking the foreign language that her mother shyly spoke. I don't know if my daughter ever heard me call my mother *umma* that time.

The hot air was so humid, the sweat dripped down from our foreheads even without the addition of steaming hot soup, but my mother made us *baeksuk* in almost 40 degrees of Italian heat. Sticky rice studded with chewy dried red jujube was perfectly starchy. It was the thing she often made back home, with needle and thread to patch up the skin of chicken to hold the rice that was stuffed in the cavity. I sorted through the grains of sticky white rice with my chopsticks, bringing them closer to my mouth and indulging in a tenderness that felt rare and precious.

Some years ago, I took my young family home to see my little sister get married. Unable to quantify our feelings in words, we shared many bowls of rice instead.

You know, people say distance makes the heart grow fonder, but I'm not sure if that's true. Maybe a short time apart is a good tonic that can revitalize a relationship, but in my case, a long time apart (building another life) so far away made my heart drift, unable hold any of it or them close. I now struggle to run to my mother the same way my child runs for me. The soft, rounded body that carried me for nine months to give me life feels strangely foreign and untouchable. I could not hug my father for the same reasons. So instead, we sit closer to eat together, to remind us that we are family, and that a family who eats together stays together.

-

NOTES ON WASHING RICE

I learnt to scrub rice anti-clockwise three times and rinse it three times more from watching my mother. She placed her pale hand gently over the washed rice to gauge the water for the perfectly steamed rice, which came up just below the first knuckle. Every grain of her rice was plump and glossy, with a gently crusted, scorched bottom when cooked on the hob.

For two servings, put 150g (5½oz/heaped ¾ cup) of short-grain white rice into a bowl of cold water and swish around quickly to separate the sitting dust or debris that will float to the surface. Drain off the water and repeat once more. After you have drained off the water for the second time, gently rub the grains to separate, then add water to rinse. Drain the starchy water carefully and repeat two more times. The water in which you rinse the rice will change from milky white to more translucent but not completely clear (more like the colour of coconut water) as you repeat the process. The water from the second or third rinsing is often saved and used to form a base stock for Everyday *Doenjang* Stew (page 116).

During the winter, washing rice can feel extremely cold and uncomfortable. One tip I've picked up along the way is to use a large balloon whisk instead – it also helps if you're not so sure how to rub the grains gently enough but also effectively.

NOTES ON RATIO OF WATER

There are many factors that influence the amount of water needed for rice. As a general rule of thumb, I use a range between 1:1 and 1:1.5 weight of dry rice to water. Fresh crop will require a little less water than old rice. If you're cooking multigrain rice, it will need closer to 1:1.5. But the amount of water also very much depends on your preference. Some might prefer the grains a little drier while others like it more sticky. So just try it out to figure out what you like best.

For example, for me, for every 150g (5½oz/scant ¾ cup) of dry, uncooked rice, I add 180ml (6fl oz/¾ cup) of cold water after the final drain. Or use the first knuckle method, which will give you a ratio of more or less 1:1.2 of rice to water that works well with white short-grain rice.

Let the rice grains soak for 30 minutes before cooking but after washing, to help the grains separate and properly hydrate.

NOTES ON COOKING RICE

Having a small rice cooker definitely makes cooking rice a doddle, though with a little practice, it is equally do-able in a pan.

Start with a heavy-based pan with a lid and add the rice and water. Bring to the boil with the lid on, then immediately turn the heat down to low–medium to cook for 10 minutes, then turn the temperature right down, as low as it goes, and let it gently steam for 5 minutes, when the rice should have fully absorbed the water. Remove from the heat and let it sit for 10 minutes, with the lid left on to steam, before serving.

Rice

Mixed Rice with Vegetables

Bibim translates as 'to mix' and *bap* means 'cooked rice'. It is essentially a rice bowl with toppings that you mix together to eat. It's a well-known Korean dish loved by all for its eye-catching visuals and deliciousness, and it happens to be incredibly nutritious, too.

What is a little less known, though, is that there are almost 10 regional varieties (think Italian ragù, for instance), showcasing countless combinations of vegetables and proteins, and each iteration shares different cooking techniques influenced by the local culture and history. Many typically utilize the seasonal ingredients more common to the regions, and restaurants specializing in regional varieties pride themselves in championing the meticulous process that respects the tradition of individually seasoning each element to create overall harmony and balance: to bring the togetherness.

I thought carefully about how best to write a recipe for such an iconic dish as *bibimbap*, and felt that it couldn't be any more apt for me to draw the attention to the culture of *bibimbap* at home, focusing on how the bowl is built in practice, rather than as a single recipe.

At home, it is not always an elaborate affair of a number of different vegetables and proteins, though they are usually thoughtfully curated to give both textural and visual contrast. Often, the dish is influenced by odds and ends of *namul* ('seasoned vegetables') from *banchan* dishes that need eating. It can be as simple as just one *namul*, such as Spicy Radish Salad (page 36) thrown into a bowl with a gnarly fried egg with a perfectly runny yolk. All you need is a good dollop of straight up *gochujang* paste and a drizzle of gorgeously aromatic toasted sesame oil to bind everything together. It can be as simple or as complex as you want it to be: completely adaptable.

Soy sauce-seasoned dried shiitake mushrooms are really flavoursome and have a pleasant chewiness that adds an interesting texture to the dish – and it's a brilliant way to used up already rehydrated mushrooms from making stocks (page 219 or 220). Vinegar-marinated carrots are my go-to filling – these are also great for Three-Coloured Seaweed Rice Roll (page 169) – which are sautéed just enough to soften and finished with subtle acidity to bring the brightness.

Serves 2

Topping suggestions
Sautéed Courgettes
 (page 24)
Sautéed Radish (page 26)
Spicy Radish Salad
 (page 36)
Beansprout Salad – Two
 Ways (page 39)
Seasoned Spinach Salad
 (page 40)
Spring Bitter Greens with
 Doenjang (page 41)

For the mushrooms
4 rehydrated dried shiitake
 mushrooms, reserving
 4 tbsp of the soaking
 water
1 tbsp soy sauce
2 tsp mirin
½ tsp golden granulated
 sugar
¼ tsp freshly cracked
 black pepper
1 garlic clove, minced
1 tsp toasted sesame oil
½ tbsp vegetable oil
4 tbsp mushroom soaking
 water, or water

For the carrots
1 tbsp extra virgin olive oil
200g (7oz) carrots,
 julienned
sea salt flakes, to season
1 tbsp mirin
1 tbsp rice wine vinegar

For the eggs
3 tbsp extra virgin olive oil
2 eggs

To finish
300g (10½oz/1½ cups)
 cooked short-grain
 Korean rice
toasted sesame oil
gochujang or Stir-Fried
 Gochujang Sauce
 (page 224), to taste

For the mushrooms, squeeze the excess water out and reserve the mushroom water. Thinly slice the mushrooms, including the stalks – they are perfectly edible – and place in a small mixing bowl. Add the soy sauce, mirin, sugar, black pepper, garlic and sesame oil. Let it marinate for 10 minutes or so, while you cook the carrots. You can come back to the mushrooms after the carrots to cook them in the same pan.

For the carrots, heat the olive oil in a sauté pan over a medium heat. Add the carrots and sauté gently for a couple of minutes with a good pinch of salt. You should notice the tint of deep orangey yellow seeping into the oil and smelling quite fragrant. Remove from the heat when the carrots appear softened. Transfer the carrots to a bowl while hot. Add the mirin and vinegar. Combine well and cover the bowl with a plate to let it further steam and marinate in the residual heat.

Rice

Now return to the mushrooms. Heat the vegetable oil in the same pan you fried the carrots, over a medium heat. Add the marinated mushrooms to the pan and sauté gently for 2 minutes. You will notice the smell of garlic and sweet soy sauce. Add 3 tablespoons of the reserved mushroom soaking water (or just plain water) to the pan. Let it come to a gentle bubble, then lower the heat. Simmer for 10 minutes, or until the mushrooms have absorbed all the liquid. They should look glossy and plump. Check for seasoning. You may want to add a little salt or a touch more sugar. Remove from the heat.

To fry the eggs, heat the olive oil in a frying pan (skillet) for a couple of minutes over a medium heat. You want the oil to get nice and hot but not smoking, so that when you crack the eggs in they sizzle.

Crack the eggs in, ensuring they are not too close. Let them fry for 2 minutes without touching, then tilt the pan slightly away from you to pool the oil, and carefully baste around the whites that still appear raw. Keep the yolks nice and runny. You should have perfectly fried eggs with crispy edges. Remove from the heat.

To serve, divide the warm steamed rice into individual bowls. Arrange your vegetables on top, along with the fried eggs. Top with a drizzle of sesame oil and serve with 1 tablespoon each (or less if you prefer less heat) of *gochujang* or Stir-fried *Gochujang* Sauce.

Three-Coloured Seaweed Rice Roll

Samsaek Gimbap

On the mornings of many school trips, my mother rose at the crack of dawn to roll *gimbap*, and I watched her as a child, tightly perched on the seat by her side, like a puppy waiting for a treat. I observed the way she seasoned the rice; how she julienned her carrots; how she laid the fillings. Her fingertips were glistening and perfumed deliciously with toasted sesame oil, she pinched and pressed the balled rice onto the sheet of roasted dry seaweed, evenly spreading only up to about three quarters of the way. She nestled the handful of bright orange carrots and grassy green spinach on top of batons of luminous-yellow, sweet pickled radish and warm salty ham, and thin crêpe-like omelettes that were separated into yellow and white ribbons. Tucking everything in together tightly to roll, she held and lifted everything in one smooth pull and tuck, before finishing it off with a lick of sesame oil and seeds. My mother always ate the knobbly end bits, offering me the perfectly shaped second slice; often adding that I should eat only the beautiful things.

Gimbap was one of the early Korean dishes I started making for my daughter, albeit less elaborately; always offered to her without the knobbly ends because I want my child to eat only the nicest things. It often makes me curious that my mother might have felt the same kind of devotion, heavily embellished with somewhat overwhelming responsibilities. I feel a lot of her gentle love that went into making *gimbap* and how she might have treasured the ordinary moments of her child keenly watching her as she cooked.

I am a firm believer that making a good *gimbap* depends on how well you cook and season the rice. The rice should not be too wet and should not taste bland, but should rather have a pronounced savoury taste, seasoned with a touch of toasted sesame oil, salt and with or without sesame seeds. After that, you can pretty much stuff it with anything you like and roll away.

More typical fillings such as pickled daikon radish (*danmuji*) can be found in Korean supermarkets, sold whole or cut into perfectly sized batons for *gimbap* making. You will also come across more conveniently packed combinations of *danmuji* and braised burdock roots together. The recipe here is merely a suggestion to get you started, so do get creative with whatever fillings you like.

Makes 4 rolls

Seasoned Spinach Salad
(page 40)

For the eggs
3 eggs
sea salt flakes
1 tbsp vegetable oil

For the carrots
1 tbsp extra virgin olive oil
200g (7oz) carrots, julienned
sea salt flakes, to season
1 tbsp mirin
1 tbsp rice wine vinegar

For the rice
600g (1lb 7oz/3 cups)
   freshly cooked white
   short-grain rice
1 tbsp toasted sesame oil,
   plus extra for brushing
2 tsp sea salt flakes

For rolling and finishing
4 sheets of seaweed
toasted white sesame
   seeds for garnish
   (optional)

Prepare the seasoned spinach salad according to the recipe.

In a small mixing bowl, lightly whisk the eggs with a generous pinch of salt.

Heat the vegetable oil in a non-stick frying pan (skillet) over a low heat and gently pour in the whisked eggs, making sure they spread out as thinly and evenly as possible. You will notice the top drying and the edge starting to set. Let it cook for a minute or two until the centre of the egg appears almost set, then carefully flip it over and cook for another 10 seconds on the other side. Transfer to a chopping board.

Fold the egg sheet gently and julienne very thinly. Set aside.

→

For the carrots, wipe down the same frying pan with kitchen paper and heat the olive oil over a medium heat. Add the carrots and sauté gently for a couple of minutes with a good pinch of salt until they smell quite fragrant. Remove from the heat when the carrots appear softened. Transfer the carrots to a bowl while hot. Add the mirin and rice wine vinegar. Combine well and cover the bowl with a plate to let it further steam and marinate in the residual heat.

Place the warm cooked rice into a large mixing bowl, along with the sesame oil and sea salt. Using a rice paddle or spatula, stir energetically but gently so that you coat each grain of rice with the seasoning without mushing the rice; folding from the edges to the middle of the bowl is a good way to keep things moving evenly. The rice should be slightly cooled down, enough to handle comfortably with bare hands. Check the seasoning and add a pinch more salt, if necessary.

To roll the *gimbap*, it is not essential to have the traditional bamboo mat known in Korean as a *gimbal*, though it can provide stability. You can use a sheet of thick foil if needed, but honestly, it really isn't too difficult after a few practice runs. Just be confident with the first lift and tuck and it will all be fine. Think of rolling a sheet of paper into a tight tube.

Place a sheet of seaweed on a chopping board or a bamboo mat, if using, shiny-side down. You want the shorter edges to become the width laid in front of you. Have a small bowl of water nearby. Scoop 150g (5½oz/¾ cup) of rice onto the centre of the seaweed. Wet your

fingertips a little and start spreading the rice as evenly as possible, pinching and pressing firmly onto the seaweed. The rice should start 1cm (½in) away from the bottom edge closest to you, and finish 2.5cm (1in) from the farthest end. Make sure you spread the rice to the full width of the sheet. The rice layer doesn't need to be thick.

Arrange the filling ingredients in a line in the centre of the rice. It doesn't really matter in which order you build the filling; it's more important that the fillings are positioned centrally on the rice, rather than the sheet of seaweed.

Position both hands over the filling with thumbs gently lifting the edges of seaweed closest to you. In one smooth motion, confidently lift the edge and fold to encase the filling, pressing down the edges firmly onto the rice. Tuck everything in firmly with a gentle cupping motion, with your fingertips pressing down the edges you just folded. It should already feel quite firm. Then simply roll away with the same cupping motion, until you reach the end. You can dab some water at the end if the edges of the seaweed do not stick. Repeat the process until you have four seaweed rolls.

Brush the finished rolls with a touch of sesame oil. Wet the blade of your sharp knife with a little water as you go along to keep the slices nice and clean It is usually sliced into about 2cm (¾in) thick, bite-sized pieces. Sprinkle with a few sesame seeds, if you like, and serve immediately – *gimbap* is best eaten fresh.

Curried Pot Rice

Growing up, one of my favourite things about my mother making curry was having the leftovers the next day. A small amount of thick, congealed gravy did not look particularly appetizing to the eye, with nothing much to show other than a few remaining bits of cubed vegetables that were completely softened into the sauce. But the barely there potatoes were enticingly creamy, onions so small and so sweet, and although tinged with brown more than luminously vivid green, garden peas still burst their pop of brightness.

And even with no evidence of meat in sight, I would gladly tuck into the mildly spiced mud of sauce, gently heated up to just warm, smooshing it into a hot bowl of rice to bind everything together into a gloriously warming bowl of something entirely different. The sauce wasn't enough to make everything wet, but rather perfect to give the rice the gentle curry flavour. I used to eat this with a fried egg on top and a dollop of just-about-sour kimchi accompanying each and every spoonful. It tasted absolutely heavenly.

So this is an ode to that leftover affair of bright yellow Korean curry that my mother used to make with ready-made Ottogi curry powder: made in one pot with nothing much to show for it other than divinely flavoured golden rice. Eat with kimchi.

Serves 4

300g (10½oz) white
    short-grain rice
300ml (10fl oz/1¼ cups)
    water or chicken stock
1 tbsp soy sauce
1 tbsp coriander seeds
1 tsp cumin seeds
½ tsp black peppercorns
¼ tsp fenugreek seeds
½ tsp Kashmiri chilli
    powder
1 tsp ground turmeric
2 tbsp vegetable oil
½ onion, thinly sliced
20g (¾oz) unsalted butter
3 garlic cloves, finely
    minced
200g (7oz) tomatoes,
    skinned and roughly
    chopped
1 tsp golden granulated
    sugar
2 tsp sea salt flakes
100g (3½oz) frozen peas

To finish
2 tsp snipped chives

Place the uncooked rice into a mixing bowl and wash thoroughly (page 164). Once the water starts to run clear, fill the bowl with cold water and soak the rice for 30 minutes, then drain the rice, using a fine sieve. In a small jug, measure out the water or stock and mix with the soy sauce. Have them ready near the stove.

Meanwhile, place the coriander seeds, cumin seeds, black peppercorns and fenugreek seeds in a small saucepan and dry roast over a low heat for a minute or so to activate the aromas. Swivel the pan around a little to keep the spices moving. It should smell very fragrant but not burnt. Once the whole spices are roasted, grind them to a fine powder using either a spice grinder or a mortar and pestle. Stir in the chilli powder and turmeric. Set aside.

Heat the vegetable oil in a heavy-based, lidded saucepan over a low heat. Add the onions along with a good pinch of salt, and sauté gently to caramelize for about 10–15 minutes. Stir frequently. The onions should turn completely floppy and beautifully caramelized, with the edges catching a little colour. If you feel it is cooking too fast, add a tiny splash of water.

Once the onions are jammy, melt in the butter. Stir in the garlic and spice mix, and cook for a minute or two so the garlic and spices can soften into the caramelized onion. Add the tomatoes, sugar and salt, then cook for 5 minutes. Stir in the drained rice, water and soy sauce. Put the lid on and simmer for 10 minutes over a low–medium heat.

Turn the heat down as low as it can go. Add the peas on top. Put the lid back on and cook for a further 8 minutes to steam. Turn off the heat and let it sit for 10 minutes with the lid firmly left on. Once 10 minutes are up, carefully open the lid and give it a gentle stir with a rice paddle or wooden spoon to mix it all up – you should notice the slightly crunchy crust at the bottom of the pan.

Divide the rice between bowls and scatter with snipped chives. Serve immediately while warm.

Rice

Midnight Kimchi Fried Rice for Kiki

Although I no longer remember what my mother's kimchi fried rice tasted like, I know instinctively, hers would have tasted strongly of her well-ripened kimchi, which would have been seasoned with plenty of salted fish, carrying the funky depth of umami flavour and almost refreshing effervescent tanginess. She added nothing else, but stir-fried her kimchi in plenty of oil before stirring in the rice and scrambling in the eggs. Kimchi fried rice, to me, is a taste of everyday love that feels as safe and comforting as a mother's hug and as familiar as one's mother tongue in a foreign city.

Kimchi fried rice is also the dish I often think I'd like to share with my daughter one day, to feed her midnight hunger. I fast forward the clock several times in my head and imagine the intimate scenes of our midnight feast; standing quietly in my softly lit kitchen, hovering over the stove side by side, we would frivolously dig straight in for the scorched rice at the bottom of the pan, while frantically blowing our mouths to temper the heat (both temperature and chilli) as we both know, us Koreans like to eat our food steaming hot. She might even suggest we have it with a softly oozing ball of mozzarella melted atop the unctuously chewy rice, while greedily sneaking a couple of large chunks into her mouth for every handful she scatters on top, just as she does when making pizzas with me.

I sometimes wonder, as ordinary as it seems, if something like kimchi fried rice is what she might reach out for when she misses her home, and it becomes the bridge that enables her to preserve her Koreanness.

I use the pork spread 'nduja here, which quite conveniently allows me to scoop it straight from the pack without fuss. 'Nduja is a spicy (as in chilli heat) cured pork sausage from Calabria in Southern Italy. Made from the trimmings of various meat cuts, fat and sometimes offal, it is uniquely rich in taste, spreadable in constancy and quite hot, thanks to the generous addition of local Calabrian chilli peppers. Melted into softly fried kimchi, within minutes it unleashes the heat, and the buttery texture of 'nduja really mellows into the soured kimchi to bring lip-smacking unctuousness. I like to use a skillet or frying pan instead of a wok to yield the wonderfully crispy scorched rice that crusts at the bottom of the pan. Top with a crispy olive-oil fried egg with an oozy golden yolk, which becomes a binder and offers some relief from the spiciness. Eat it straight from the pan.

Serves 2

1½ tbsp vegetable oil
200g (7oz) kimchi, roughly chopped
1 tsp golden granulated sugar
70g (2½oz) 'nduja (cured pork spread)
1 tbsp mirin
300g (10½oz/2½ cups) cooked white short-grain rice
1 tbsp soy sauce
2 tsp *gochujang* (Korean red chilli paste)
1 tsp oyster sauce
¼ tsp freshly cracked black pepper

To finish

3 tbsp extra virgin olive oil
2 eggs
2 tbsp *gim jaban* (crumbled toasted seasoned seaweed)
2 tsp toasted sesame oil

Heat the vegetable oil in a frying pan (skillet) over a medium heat. Add the kimchi and sugar and sauté for 3 minutes to soften the kimchi. Stir in the 'nduja and mirin and cook for 1 minute to incorporate. Stir in the rice followed by the soy sauce, *gochujang*, oyster sauce and black pepper. Continue frying for 3–5 minutes.

Reduce the heat and, using the back of a spatula or a large wooden spoon, spread the rice thinly and evenly around the pan, while pressing down quite firmly. Let it sit over a low heat for 3 minutes without disturbing the pan to form a light crust. Remove the pan from the heat after 3 minutes. Let it sit for a couple of minutes.

Meanwhile, to fry the eggs, heat the olive oil in a frying pan for a couple of minutes over a medium heat. You want the oil to get nice and hot but not smoking, so that when you crack the eggs in they sizzle. Crack the eggs in, ensuring they are not too close together. Let them fry for 2 minutes without touching. After 2 minutes, tilt the pan slightly away from you to pool the oil and carefully baste around any whites that still appear raw. Keep the yolk nice and runny. You should have perfectly fried eggs with a crispy edge. Remove from the heat.

Serve the rice immediately, topped with the eggs and crumbled seaweed and drizzled with the sesame oil. Eat straight from the pan to scrape off the caramelized rice at the bottom.

Mung Bean Porridge

Savoury rice porridge is often what commonly completes the spread of Chicken Soup for the Dog Days – *Baesksuk* (page 111).

A simply flavoured rice porridge, loosened until silky with rich chicken broth, was also the thing my mother cooked for us on the days we felt unwell to comfort us. Topped with crumbled seaweed, once stirred through, speckles of deep green-black flakes became the faint reminder of the salty sea. The perfectly softened rice was pleasantly mushy – you could just about notice the grains in a singular form – and the rich chicken-y broth felt as warm and soothing to the mind as it was on the tongue, with an occasional kick of umami coming in and out to perk up the lazy appetite.

Korean rice porridge is often loaded with finely diced vegetables along with seasonal toppings from the land and sea, but I actually much prefer the simplicity of a blank canvas that allows the depth of chicken broth to shine. Mung bean porridge is considered a real delicacy, boasting many health benefits that are believed to energize a tired body.

I like to top mine with a barely poached egg (instead of the usual garnish of shredded chicken) to bind my silky rice with creamy golden liquid. The addition of some perfectly ripe, acidic and effervescent kimchi to contrast the richness completes the beautifully balanced one-bowl magic. These are merely suggestions, rather than a fixed instruction, but don't miss out the crumbled seaweed.

Serves 4

100g (3½oz/heaped ¾ cup) glutinous rice
100g (3½oz) mung dal
2 tbsp toasted sesame oil
1.2 litres (40fl oz/4¾ cups) leftover chicken stock from *Baeksuk* (page 111)
1 tbsp soup or light soy sauce
½ tsp ground white pepper
sea salt flakes, to taste

To finish
2 tsp very thin julienne matchsticks of ginger root
4 tbsp *gim jaban* (crumbled toasted seasoned seaweed)

For the topping (optional)
poached egg
kimchi

Start the prep the night before. Begin the process by washing and soaking the rice and dal, as insufficient preparation will lead to a porridge with an unpleasant odour that tastes floury on the tongue. Place the rice and dal into a large bowl and wash them thoroughly, as you would with usual rice prep (page 164), until the water runs clear. Fill the bowl with cold water and let the rice and dal soak overnight. The following morning, using a fine sieve, drain the rice and dal and set aside.

Gently heat the sesame oil in a heavy-based saucepan over a low–medium heat. Add the drained rice and dal and sauté for a couple of minutes to coat them in the oil, stirring occasionally to stop them from sticking to the pan. You will notice fragrant aromas of sesame oil and, in a minute or two, grains of rice may start to stick a little and appear translucent.

Gradually add the stock in a few stages, so you can incorporate the rice and dal into the liquid with control.

Increase the heat a touch to bring the mixture to simmering point, then simmer gently for 45 minutes over a low heat. Stir every now and then to ensure the rice does not get stuck to the bottom of the pan. You should notice very gentle bubbles erupting through and the blip-blip sound that is not dissimilar to the sound of simmering tomato sauce. After 45 minutes, the rice and dal should have broken down into soft creamy mush, and the porridge thickened perfectly to the consistency of runny custard. Stir in the soy sauce and white pepper. Check for seasoning and add salt to taste.

To serve, divide into individual bowls. Top each bowl with a poached egg and kimchi, if using, and garnish it with a little ginger and crumbled seaweed.

Rice

Crispy Rice Cake Skewers

Tteok Kkochi

This is my all-time favourite dish of childhood, where the sky was painted in deep shades of ocean blue, and the summer evenings felt generous and bright, abundantly studded with shining stars that made me dream about tomorrow. The air was humid and sweet with magical energy and the breath of youth.

A single stick of deep-fried rice cake licked with sunset-orange ketchup glaze after school was my first taste of sugar-coated spice. The sauce so deliciously sweet and spicy from the subtle hum of *gochujang*, some children liked to lick it all off first, while if you are like me, you would have carefully bitten into the hot crispy rice cake, savouring the glaze and letting the satisfyingly chewy interior hug the tongue and make it dance with happiness.

The glaze is quite generous and you will have some left over: it keeps well for a couple of days in the fridge. Cylinder-shaped rice cakes can be found in fridge or freezer sections of Asian grocers and also online. Occasionally, if you are lucky, you may also come across freshly made rice cakes, or rice cakes made from flour. All of these will work absolutely fine. If you can only find thinly sliced ones, just omit the skewering.

Soak the wooden skewers in cold water for 30 minutes.

If you are using frozen rice cakes, soak them in cold water for 10 minutes to soften, as otherwise they will break easily. Then blanch the rice cakes in boiling water for 1 minute. Drain and rinse with cold water. Pat dry with kitchen paper to remove any excess moisture, then skewer 4 rice cakes onto each pre-soaked skewer.

Meanwhile, combine all the ingredients for the glaze in a small saucepan over a medium heat. Bring to a gentle simmer and cook for 5 minutes to thicken the sauce. Check the seasoning. It should taste assertively sweet with a gentle tanginess and background heat. Set aside.

Heat the vegetable oil in a large frying pan (skillet) over a medium heat. Carefully place the rice cake skewers into the frying pan and cook them for a couple of minutes on each side until cooked through and deliciously golden. Don't be tempted to fry the skewers at a high temperature as the moisture inside rice cakes can expand and burst (don't deep-fry). Shallow-frying at a lower temperature minimizes the risk.

Once the skewers are fried crisp and golden, remove from the heat. Brush them generously with the glaze on both sides and sprinkle with toasted sesame seeds, if using. Serve immediately while warm.

Makes 4 skewers

4 short wooden skewers
16 *tteokbokki* rice cakes, about 225g (8oz)
3 tbsp vegetable oil, for frying

For the glaze
3 tbsp tomato ketchup (catsup)
2 tbsp golden granulated sugar
1 tbsp *gochujang* (Korean red chilli paste)
1 tbsp soy sauce
1 tsp perilla oil
1 garlic clove, minced
60ml (2fl oz/¼ cup) water

To finish
liberal sprinkling of toasted white sesame seeds (optional)

Noodles

seven

a taste of my father's home arrived in summer

Seoul moves fast. Its cityscapes change quickly. Tarpaulin-roofed markets are cordoned off to become brick-built shops. Tall flashy buildings with balconies and rooftop gardens overlooking the city's dramatic landscapes arrive to gentrify the area, without anyone ever noticing the stories that once lived amongst the rubble of its past which lies beneath the earth.

My late paternal granddad was supposedly the lucky chosen one to have lived in the poorest part of Seoul, which was mapped out to be developed over the course of a few years. He escaped the north during the Korean War and found his new home in Seoul. My granddad's shabby, crumbling house, where he lived alone, sat on the edge of the higgledy-piggledy hilltop, and was only reachable via thousands of narrow, uneven steps. People dressed in suits kept on visiting to convince him to get his home demolished in exchange for a small token gesture. His answer was always 'no'.

My father knew his way around those unnamed alleys and steep hills that surrounded the many houses he'd moved to and from in the area. I have a scar on my right arm that always reminds me of the story about one of the first houses I was supposed to have lived in as a child. My mother married my father there and took on the responsibilities of looking after my homesick granddad. My mother told me how a pot of boiling water scorched my pale baby skin red raw while she was at work. She rushed her precious baby to the hospital in tears and promised herself she would make sure that she would never have to climb those steps ever again. My grandmother would have been alive then, though I have no memories of her. I might have heard that she lived her life with a man who suffered from the aftermath of the war. My granddad drank to drown his sorrows, while my mother swallowed thousands of bitter pills in silence, for being a woman who couldn't birth a baby boy – until she finally did.

But I don't remember much of it at all.

In my fading memories, my granddad neatly folded piles of newspapers and collected empty bottles. He took a couple of plastic bagfuls to the corner shop in exchange for sweet honey-soaked ginger cookies or a bag of puffed rice, which he gave to me as a gift whenever I visited him.

I ran the long hilly roads to the playground not far from his house to play with cousins who lived nearby. And when I returned crying, with grazed knees weeping blood, my granddad wiped it all off with his bare hands and gave me sweet candies he kept in his drawer. I didn't know what being poor meant, even when my father occasionally talked about his hungry childhood eating noodles until he felt sick of them, unable to afford enough grains of rice for the whole family. I struggle to grasp the idea of poverty to that desperate degree.

When my granddad passed away, his ashes were sprinkled into the river that was believed to come from, or ran upstream to, North Korea. My father prayed for him to finally rest his soul in the water that tasted of his home. He was saddened about his father's life. The pixel-sharp image of my granddad's hollow and sorrowful eyes stayed to haunt him, even long after he grieved his loss with many tears alone in the dark.

My parents worked day and night. There was a bright spark in my father's eyes that was determined to succeed. My mother slung her babies on her back to unbox and re-box the sample sanitary pads to resell at low price to hospital staff and local friends. She put that money on the side and paid for my piano lessons and an English tutor because I said I wanted to go to America someday. Their business continued to boom and all of their hard work started to pay off. The shadow of poverty that cast across my father's face

started to soften. My mother's soft, perfectly manicured hands became the home that housed grit. Dirt gathered under their fingernails with sweat dripping down their curved backs – but so did the money.

Not long after my granddad died, we move to a fancier apartment with more rooms and bathrooms. We had flashy kitchen units with faux marble tops, and a floor-to-ceiling pantry that hoarded cereal boxes and packets of noodles. The floors were shiny and the living was easy. But I know the success always sat heavily on my father, who had hoped to help my granddad out, or maybe even to live together before he passed away. He knew he was so close.

My father ate cold northern-style *naengmyeon* noodles in summer. We went to the same restaurant and sat at the same table where we had to take our shoes off to sit cross-legged. There was a sign on the wall, directly opposite our table and next to the stairs that led to the toilets. The laminated A4 card read 'Please look after your expensive shoes, we cannot be responsible.'

My father put his tatty old shoes over my shiny red brogues and fancy designer trainers. He didn't take his eyes off them while he made an order of the same usual things: one *bibim naengmyeon* for me, four *mul naengmyeon* for the rest. He ordered a couple of plates of kimchi-stuffed northern-style dumplings from time to time, and slurped the same bowl of slushy beefy broth in the same vacant, soulful way. He often asked if I would try it. I couldn't

chew the noodles properly for fear of choking and it barely tasted of anything at all to my uneducated palate. There was a sense of unsatisfying blandness that tasted full of emotion.

Curse or blessing? My father and I seem to share the same little piece of blue heart that desperately misses the home where we once belonged. I trace my steps through the forgotten alleys of our old haunts like a ghost looking for a home to hug. Eventually, the streets in my head become recognizable enough to chase the threads that root back to the north. And at last, I can piece together the puzzle that makes my father him – and therefore also me.

I am always relieved to find the restaurant still in the same corner of the hustling and bustling market. Run by the same family since 1967, it seems to have withstood the testing times of gentrification. It's one of only a few places left in Seoul that can tell me the story of my father's smooth brown face and his cheeky banter with many people who once served at our table.

Seasons change and nothing ever looks the same. But the smell in the air is always delicious, laced with nose-tingling mustard and vinegar. The taste buds on my tongue remind me of all the small things that used to make this place feel so ordinary but also so special. And now I know, this place could have been the only thing that reminded him of my granddad and his long-lost home.

Buckwheat Noodles in Icy Pink Broth

If *bibim naengmyeon* (page 188) was the bold and loud energy of the young and vibrant extrovert, I think *mul naengmyeon* is the tastefully demure elegance of the introvert. Modest in its appearance, a soft nest of springy buckwheat noodles drenched in ice-cold broth; the river of barely frozen slushy liquid quenches the thirst and cools down the body from the inside to rescue you from the sweltering heat of the Korean summer.

Traditionally, a mixture of beef brisket and shin is simmered together for hours, with the addition of beef bones to yield the depth, then meticulously processed to remove the fat to ensure clarity, before being combined with tangy juice from Radish Water Kimchi to establish the balance. It is nuanced delicately with subtle acidity and the effervescence of ferment which are then personalized once more with the nose-tickling heat of mustard and vinegar you add at the table, as you wish. It eats delicately and boasts a refreshing finish that can come across as almost bland, with a bewildering lack of flavour.

The dish usually demands a couple of days to process, thus this is not the sort of thing home cooks often make from scratch; in fact, it is a lot cheaper to buy it from a restaurant in Korea.

What we have here isn't the traditional beefy broth but rather a relatively easy fix to satisfy the cravings on a hot day – providing you are well equipped with water kimchi.

Water Kimchi (page 83) will need about five days to ferment perfectly for the dish, and the Beetroot-Stained Vinegar-Pickled Radish (page 90) will need a couple of days to take on a decent level of sourness. Serve the broth ice cold straight from the freezer, preferably partially frozen.

Naengmyeon noodles can be found in Asian grocers and online; they are springy and have a particularly resistant chewiness which can be tricky to bite through, so they are best served with scissors to cut them before eating. In case you find them difficult to source, thin soba noodles will make a suitable substitution.

Serves 2

250ml (9fl oz/1 cup) cold water
3 tbsp cider vinegar
1 tbsp *yondu* (seasoning sauce)
1 tsp English mustard
250ml (9fl oz/1 cup) juice from Water Kimchi (page 83)

For the topping
80g (3oz) Beetroot-Stained Vinegar-Pickled Radish (page 90)
1 hard-boiled (hard-cooked) egg, peeled and halved

To finish
2 servings of *naengmyeon* noodles
toasted white sesame seeds

Combine the cold water with the vinegar, *yondu*, mustard and the juice from the water kimchi and stir well. Transfer to a freezer-safe container. Chill in the freezer for a couple of hours until partially frozen. Alternatively, store it in the fridge.

Before you are ready to serve, prepare the toppings; now is also a good time to boil the egg.

Bring a large pan of water to a rapid boil and cook the noodles according to the packet instructions. *Naengmyeon* noodles overcook very easily, so do keep an eye on them. Carefully drain the noodles and rinse well under cold running water a few times to remove the starch, using a scrubbing motion with your hands. Drain thoroughly, then divide the noodles into two bowls, add the radish pickles and put a halved egg on top. Carefully divide the chilled broth among the bowls and sprinkle with toasted sesame seeds.

COLD NOODLES

COLD NOODLES

Chilled Noodle Soup with Charred Aubergine

Gaji Naengguksu

The concept of chilled noodle soup may sound a little strange and unfamiliar to some, but in Korea, temperatures rise steadily to hit highs of 30 degrees in summer with intense humidity. And noodles served in ice-cold broth can really hit the spot to revive the tired body and mind.

Simple broth made with dried kelp is seasoned lightly here to keep it delicate and refreshing. The flavours from wonderfully smoky charred aubergines marinated in piquant soy sauce erupt amongst the gentle waves of cooling liquid to contrast the broth and soft noodles beautifully with its slightly bitter edge (in a good way) – the aubergines alone are worth a try.

I like to pair it with thin dried wheat noodles; their delicate nature and neutral flavour complements the rest of the components. If unavailable, try with buckwheat noodles (soba noodles) instead.

Serves 4

For the broth
650ml (23fl oz/2¾ cups) Quick Stock (page 219)
1 tsp golden granulated sugar
1 tsp soup or light soy sauce
1 tsp sea salt flakes, or to taste
2 tsp cider vinegar

For the aubergines (eggplants)
2 aubergines, about 700g (1lb 9oz), sliced into 1cm (½in) thick discs
1 tbsp vegetable oil, for brushing
sea salt flakes, to season
2 tsp thin julienne matchsticks of ginger root
1 garlic clove, minced
1 red bird's eye chilli, chopped
1 green bird's eye chilli, chopped
2 tbsp cider vinegar
2 tbsp mirin
1 tbsp golden caster (superfine) sugar
1 tbsp soy sauce
1 tbsp toasted sesame oil
½ tsp *gochugaru* (Korean red chilli flakes)

For the noodles
4 servings of *somyeon* or *somen* noodles (thin dried wheat noodles)
½ red onion, thinly sliced, soaked in cold water for 10 minutes
2 spring onions (scallions), sliced
1 tsp toasted white sesame seeds

To make the broth, combine all the ingredients in a jug or bottle and refrigerate until needed.

If you want to serve the broth icy cold and slushy, transfer the broth to the freezer about 30 minutes before serving.

Preheat the griddle pan until nice and hot. Brush the sliced aubergines with a little oil (I only do it on one side to get it going) and season with a good pinch of salt. Cook the aubergines for 3–4 minutes on each side until they're softened and char marks are visible. You may need to cook the aubergines in batches. Transfer the charred aubergines to a large mixing bowl, cover and let them steam for 10 minutes – they should appear soft and more relaxed. Add the rest of the ingredients for the aubergines and toss gently to combine. Leave to marinate for a further 10 minutes to soak up the flavour.

Cook the noodles according to the packet instructions. Rinse to remove the starch, then drain thoroughly. Divide the noodles and marinated aubergines among four bowls. Gently pour the chilled broth over the noodles – about 160ml (5½fl oz/¼ cup) per bowl. Top with the red onion, spring onions and sesame seeds.

Spicy Cold Noodles

This dish of spicy cold noodles is what I would eagerly reach out for on a hot day to temper the lethargic energy and somewhat grumpy mood that seem to follow the rising temperature. Originating from the small coastal town in north Korea, thin noodles made from sweet potato starch are served cold, doused liberally in a ladleful of crimson red sauce. Its fiery heat, which comes from the copious amount of smoky chilli pepper flakes, is loud and bold, but made enjoyable, balanced with a sweet and fruity finish.

The sauce for this should really be made in advance, as *gochugaru* needs time to swell to soak up the flavour, and alliums certainly benefit from maturing in the fridge to mellow. The batch here makes about 240g (8½oz), which is more than you need for two portions; leftover sauce can be used for stir-fries or as a base for any spicy braise. Stored in airtight container, it will keep for about seven days in the fridge.

Serves 2

For the sauce
1 tbsp soft light
   brown sugar
2 tbsp soy sauce
1 tsp sliced ginger root
60ml (2fl oz/¼ cup) water
2.5 × 4cm (1 × 1.5in) piece
   of *dasima* (dried kelp)
40g (1½oz) apple, peeled
   and roughly chopped
   – use a sweet variety
   such as fuji or gala
40g (1½oz) Asian pear,
   peeled, cored and
   roughly chopped
¼ onion, roughly chopped
2 garlic cloves, minced
30g (1oz) *gochugaru*
   (Korean red
   pepper flakes)
2 tbsp cider vinegar
2 tbsp toasted sesame oil
1 tbsp clear honey
1 tsp sea salt flakes

For the topping
60g (2oz) Beetroot-
   Stained-Vinegar
   Pickled Radish
   (page 90)
60g (2oz) cucumber,
   julienned
¼ Asian pear, peeled,
   cored and thinly
   sliced (optional)
1 hard-boiled (hard-
   cooked) egg, halved

To finish
1 tbsp toasted white
   sesame seeds
2 servings of *naengmyeon*
   noodles
160ml (5½fl oz/⅔cup)
   lemon-lime flavoured
   fizzy soft drink (such
   as 7up or Sprite)

Make the sauce by combining the sugar, soy sauce and ginger in a small saucepan with the water and *dasima*. Bring to a gentle simmer, not a boil, and let it brew very gently for 15 minutes until the sugar has fully dissolved and the flavour of *dasima* has been extracted. When done, remove from the heat. Discard the *dasima* and leave the liquid to cool.

Place the apple, pear, onion and garlic into a food processor. Add the cooled soy sauce liquid, including the ginger slices. Blend to break down to a smooth purée. Add the *gochugaru*, vinegar, sesame oil, honey and salt. Blend again until smooth. Transfer to an airtight container and refrigerate for at least an hour or preferably for three days so the flavours can deepen.

Prepare the toppings and set aside. Lightly grind the sesame seeds in a pestle and mortar.

Bring a large pan of water to a rapid boil and cook the noodles according to the packet instructions. *Naengmyeon* noodles overcook very easily; when the foam and bubbles rise to the surface, it is a good sign that the noodles are done. Carefully drain the noodles and rinse well under cold running water a few times to remove the starch, using a scrubbing motion with your hands.

Drain thoroughly, then divide the noodles between two bowls. Ladle the sauce liberally on top (about 4–5 tablespoons each), followed by the toppings. Finish it off with the ground sesame seeds and lemon-lime flavoured soft drink. Mix everything together thoroughly before eating.

COLD NOODLES

Spicy Seafood Noodle Soup

Jjamppong

Jjamppong, along with *jjajangmyeon* is one of the most popular Korean Chinese dishes. For many years, it was believed to have been first introduced by Chinese immigrants in Japan who later brought it to Korea. However, there is another theory about the possible origins of the dish, which suggests that it was inspired by a Chinese dish called *chao ma mian*, which was developed by the Chinese immigrants from Shandong province who mostly ran restaurants in Korea. Although originally the dish wasn't red or spicy, it is said that an adapted version using *gochugaru* to suit the Koreans' love for spicy food gained more popularity and became known as the *jjamppong* we recognize now.

The broth, seasoned simply with *gochugaru* and soy sauce, carries gently rising heat that makes your nose tickle a little, with sweetness from the vegetables and seafood bringing the dish a sense of cooling depth to balance the flavour. It tastes incredibly complex, yet is actually quite straightforward to make at home. I use the shells and heads from the prawns to make the base stock to layer the chicken stock, but if you want to take a short cut, you could simply use chicken stock; good-quality shop-bought chicken stock is perfectly fine, if you don't have any homemade stashed away in the freezer.

I think the success of the dish depends on sufficient stir-frying of the vegetables to intensify and release flavour, so that when you add the stock, the soup doesn't become watery. Fresh wheat noodles work best here, if you can get hold of them; try not to use dried noodles that are too thin. Alternatively, omit the noodles and serve alongside fried rice as a soup – like they often do in Korean Chinese restaurants.

Serves 2

200g (7oz) clams, scrubbed
200g (7oz) mussels, scrubbed and beards removed
80g (3oz) squid, cleaned
6 fresh, raw prawns (shrimp), shell-on

For the base stock
½ tbsp vegetable oil
½ onion, roughly chopped
1 tsp thickly sliced ginger root
550ml (18fl oz/2¼ cups) water
two 5 × 7.5cm (2 × 3in) pieces of *dasima* (dried kelp)
500ml (17fl oz/2 cups) chicken stock

For the vegetables
2 spring onions (scallions), white and green parts separated
2 tbsp vegetable oil
1 tbsp perilla oil
4 garlic cloves, finely minced
3 leaves of napa cabbage, sliced into large bite-sized pieces
80g (3oz) courgettes (zucchini), halved and sliced lengthways
30g (1oz) carrot, julienned
¼ onion, thinly sliced
1½ tbsp *gochugaru* (Korean red pepper flakes)
2 tbsp light soy sauce
¼ tsp ground white pepper
sea salt flakes, to season
2 servings of wheat noodles

Purge the scrubbed clams and mussels in heavily salted water, if necessary. Discard any of the shellfish that remain open. Squid can be gutted and cleaned by the fishmonger. Once cleaned, slice it in half lengthways to open it out flat and score the inside of the squid in a criss-cross pattern, then slice it into bite-size pieces. For the prawns, remove the shells and heads, and devein. Reserve the shells and heads for the stock. Refrigerate the prepared seafood until needed.

In a small saucepan, heat the vegetable oil over a medium heat. Add the prawn shells and heads, along with the onion and sliced ginger. Cook them for 5 minutes until the shells and heads starts to colour, stirring frequently to stop them from sticking. Press down on the prawn heads with the back of

a wooden spoon or potato masher to release the flavour. Carefully stir in the water to deglaze the pan and add the *dasima*. Simmer over a low heat for 30 minutes – you may occasionally need to skim off the scum that rises to the top. After 30 minutes, strain the prawn stock through a fine sieve into a clean saucepan, and combine with the chicken stock. You should have about 800ml (28fl oz/3½ cups) of stock altogether. It is best to keep the stock warm, barely simmering, which helps to extract the flavour from the vegetables far better than cold water.

Noodles

189

Meanwhile, roughly chop the whites of the spring onions. Cut the green parts into 5cm (2in) batons and slice diagonally and very thinly. Submerge the greens in cold water for 5 minutes to remove any harshness and to wash off any slimy mucus. Set both aside.

Have all the ingredients ready, within easy reach, as the cooking process is quick.

Heat the vegetable oil in a wok over a high heat to get it nice and hot. Swiftly add the perilla oil, the white parts of the spring onions and the garlic. Stir energetically to release the flavour of the allium without burning. This should take no more than 30 seconds. Once it starts to smell fragrant, add the cabbage, courgettes, carrot and onion slices. Stir-fry the vegetables for 5 minutes, maintaining the high heat. Add a splash of water halfway through if the pan appears too hot, which will also help to draw the moisture out of the vegetables, especially the cabbage. After 5 minutes, stir in the *gochugaru* and continue stir-frying for 2–3 minutes.

Pour in the light soy sauce around the edge of the wok and stir in the white pepper. Add the stock and bring to a rapid boil before adding the clams, mussels, squid slices and prawns. After 3 minutes, the seafood should have cooked through. Discard any clams or mussels that remain closed. Check for seasoning and adjust it with a pinch of salt, if necessary.

Meanwhile, cook the noodles according to the packet instructions. Divide the noodles between the two bowls and ladle the hot soup over the noodles, ensuring each bowl has a generous amount of vegetables and seafood. Top with beautifully curled green spring onions and slurp while steaming hot.

Knife-Cut Noodles in Spicy Tomato Broth

Jang Kalguksu

The weather seems to play an influential role in Korea, dictating what to eat or what one must eat. Less pleasant elements such as bitterly cold winters or the perpetually humid and damp rainy season often unanimously call for a brothy dish with a *kal-kal-han mat* to restore warmth, which loosely translates as 'heat or texture that tickles the back of the throat'. It isn't a taste as such, but rather the taste sensation received through the body, or a mouthfeel.

This lesser-known noodle dish is regarded as a perfect antidote for those nose-biting wintry days. It originates from the mountainous region that sits north-east of South Korea, where the mountainous landscape and cooler climate makes it harder to farm. But beautiful things do happen with limitations, with locals adapting and utilizing the elements to work in their favour to produce varieties of *jangs* that are fermented long and slow, thus developing incredible depth of flavour.

The simple broth seasoned assertively with fermented chilli paste can shout intense heat, but soon tapers down to reveal a rounder, richer savoury taste that awards the dish a good body.

I rather inauthentically add tomatoes in here to tease the flavours, with an equally unusual garnish of fried leek to bring a subtle layer of bitter umami. Naturally sweet and gentle, the acidity of tomato pairs really well with chilli and brings a touch of brightness; it is so delicious!

The process is fairly straightforward but does require a bit of time and planning. I find making the dough in advance and part prepping the stock the night before helpful; it makes things far less of a daunting task.

Serves 4

For the noodle dough
125g (4oz/1 cup) plain (all-purpose) flour, plus extra for dusting
125g (4oz/1 cup) strong white bread flour
½ tsp fine sea salt
110ml (3½fl oz/scant ½ cup) water
1 tbsp vegetable oil

For the broth
1.2 litres (40fl oz/4¾ cups) *Dasima* and Mushroom Stock (page 220) or Anchovy Stock (page 221)
300g (10½oz) ripe tomatoes, skinned and quartered

For the seasoning paste
2 tbsp *gochugaru* (Korean red pepper flakes)
1 tbsp mirin
2 tbsp soy sauce
4 tbsp *gochujang* (Korean red chilli paste)
1 tbsp *doenjang* (Korean fermented bean paste)
1 tbsp fish sauce
3 garlic cloves, minced

To finish
3 tbsp vegetable oil
40g (1½oz) leek, julienned
4 tbsp *gim jaban* (crumbled toasted seasoned seaweed)
1 tbsp toasted white sesame seeds, lightly crushed

To make the noodles, place both flours in a large mixing bowl, along with the salt. Make a well in the middle and gradually pour the water and a tablespoon of oil into the well. Using chopsticks or the long handle of a wooden spoon, stir to combine the dry and wet ingredients, until you have what resembles rough crumbs. Gently knead the mix for 5 minutes or so, bringing the crumbs together to form a dough. Don't worry if the dough still appears rough in places, as we will knead it once more after the short rest. Place the dough in a reusable plastic bag or wrap with clingfilm (plastic wrap). Rest for 10 minutes at room temperature.

Return to the dough after 10 minutes. Place the dough onto a stable surface and start kneading again, energetically pressing and stretching with the heels of your hands. Continue until the dough feels supple and the surface appears smooth. It may take around 10–15 minutes. Cover the dough again with a reusable plastic bag or clingfilm, and refrigerate for at list for 1 hour or preferably overnight.

Meanwhile, prepare your choice of stock following the instructions on pages 220–221. When done, strain through a fine sieve into a large saucepan big enough to cook the noodles – you will need 1.2 litres (40fl oz/1¾ cups). Set aside for the time being.

→

Remove the dough from the fridge 30 minutes before you are ready to roll it. Divide the dough in half, so you have a more manageable volume to work with. Lightly flour your surface and start rolling out the piece into a sheet around 2–3mm (⅛in) thick. You may need to lightly dust the dough with flour as you work – do so generously before folding to ensure the sheet doesn't stick to itself. Gently fold the sheet in thirds, as you would with folding a letter. Cut the noodles into about 5mm (¼in) thick strips, then ruffle them lightly to unfold and shake off the excess flour. Repeat with the second piece of dough. Transfer the noodles onto a wide flat tray, cover with a tea towel and refrigerate until needed.

Heat the remaining vegetable oil in a saucepan over a medium heat and fry the leeks until golden and crispy. Remove the leeks from the oil and transfer to a plate lined with kitchen paper. Set aside until needed. Reserve the oil for the next step.

Add the *gochugaru* to the same saucepan and place it over a low heat, stirring continuously to move the *gochugaru* around to stop it from burning. Within half a minute or less, you will notice bubbles form and the fine chilli flakes start to swell and bloom fragrantly. Remove from the heat and add the mirin, soy sauce, *gochujang*, *doenjang*, fish sauce and garlic. Combine well and set aside.

Place the pan of strained stock over a low heat. Bring to a gentle simmer and stir in the seasoning paste. Bring to the boil. Add the tomatoes and simmer for 20 minutes until they have softened into the broth. Check the seasoning and adjust it with a pinch of salt, if necessary. Increase the heat to bring it back to a rapid boil. Shake off the excess flour from the noodles and cook the noodles directly in the broth, stirring once or twice. It should only take a couple of minutes for the noodles to cook through.

When ready, divide the noodles among four deep bowls and ladle the hot broth over the top. Top with the fried leeks, crumbled seaweed and sesame seeds. Serve immediately while steaming hot.

Noodles

Black Bean Sauce Noodles

Jjajangmyeon

Jjajangmyeon is a popular Korean Chinese dish which has firmly established itself as one of the most convenient delivery meals of all time in Korea. Every town and every apartment block have their own specialist restaurants which can deliver the bowl of comfort that reveals slippery noodles lying low beneath the grease-licked ragù-like sauce. Its glossy onyx-black sauce is decisively sweet, laced with the savoury funk of salty fermented black bean sauce. The flavours linger on, spreading wide across lips tinted with black-stained grease, and the taste buds on the tongue pull you back to have another slurp; it is completely moreish.

Sweet vegetables are essential for it to do its magic; to balance the richness of the pork and salty *chunjang* – a Korean style of black bean paste made from fermented soybeans, which can be found in Asian grocers or online.

In its raw state, besides its obvious salty notes, *chunjang* tastes slightly bitter and sour, so it is always advisable to fry off the paste in oil before cooking to neutralize it which, in turn, brings out a more rounded flavour.

Place the vegetable oil and *chunjang* in a cold wok or sauté pan over a low heat to slowly warm them up together. Stir constantly and fry off the paste for about 3 minutes until bubbles surface on top. You will notice the deeply funky and salty smell of the paste. Once done, separate the fried paste and oil – you should have about 2½ tablespoons of oil. Set both aside. We will use the oil to cook the onions.

Wipe down the pan and heat the reserved oil. Stir in the sliced spring onion whites and cook for 1–2 minutes over a medium heat until they sizzle and smell fragrant. Add the garlic, ginger, pork and a good pinch of salt, and stir-fry for about 3 minutes to brown the pork while energetically moving the pan to stop the alliums from burning. Once the pork has browned, crank up the heat and add the onions. Stir-fry the onions over a high heat for a couple of minutes to soften and caramelize. The onions should still have a little bite to them and not be completely mushy. Add the cabbage and courgette to the pan and continue cooking for a further 3 minutes or until the vegetables are softened.

Stir in the sugar, then carefully pour the soy sauce around the edge of the wok to season the onions. Add the reserved fried *chunjang* and the oyster sauce. Continue tossing and stirring vigorously to loosen and mix the paste in with the onions.

After a couple of minutes, the onions should be well coated with the thick black paste. Add the stock or water. Bring it up to the boil, then reduce the heat and simmer for 5 minutes.

Meanwhile, combine the tablespoon of water with the potato flour to make a slurry. Maintain the gentle heat and gradually stir in the slurry to thicken the sauce slightly – I find about 2 teaspoons are enough for a ragù-like consistency. Cook for a minute or two to bring it all together. Check for seasoning and adjust it with a pinch more salt and sugar, if necessary.

Cook the noodles according to the packet instructions. Divide the noodles between two bowls and ladle the warm black bean sauce over the noodles. Top with julienned cucumber, the boiled egg and pinch of chilli flakes, if using.

Serves 2 generously

4 tbsp vegetable oil
4 tbsp *chunjang* (Korean black bean paste)
2 spring onions (scallions), white parts only, thinly sliced
2 garlic cloves, finely minced
½ tsp grated ginger root
150g (5½oz) pork shoulder or belly, diced
sea salt flakes
2 small onions, diced
150g (5½oz) white cabbage, diced
70g (2½oz) courgettes (zucchini), diced
1 tbsp golden granulated sugar
1 tbsp soy sauce
2 tsp oyster sauce
250ml (9fl oz/1 cup) warm chicken stock or water
1 tbsp water
1 tsp potato flour (starch)
2 servings of wheat noodles

For the toppings
60g (2oz) cucumber, cut into julienne strips
1 soft-boiled egg, halved
pinch of fine chilli flakes (optional)

Hand-Torn Noodles in Clam Broth

If a bowl of steaming pearly white rice was an ordinary joy of everyday sustenance, noodles were a novelty weekend affair that carried our busy hands through the slower Sundays. Sitting in front of the boring old daytime family movie, my father kneaded the dough to the sound of sleepy pitter patter rain, while my mother stood lovingly by the steaming pot of ocean-scented stock. Clouds of soft, chewy dough floated in the sweet and salty umami liquid that was thickened creamily by the potatoes that had tenderly collapsed into the broth. A beautiful mess of pillowy comfort that swelled in the stomach and radiated warmth, to make you want to slouch into the sofa and drift into a long and unplanned nap. I cannot think of anything more glorious on a rainy day.

The use of pasta flour may seem strange, but it contains a very similar protein content to the Korean flour typically used for the noodles, which makes pasta flour an ideal and readily available swap.

While more traditionally the dough is flaked directly into the soup, I do find the process somewhat unreliable if you want to achieve consistent results, as the first dropped noodles will inevitably float up way before you finish working through the dough, unless you are very quick. To rectify this, I opt for roughly sheeting the dough into reasonably wide strips, then tearing them either beforehand, as written here, or directly into the broth.

Serves 2

For the noodle dough
160g (5½oz/heaped 1¼ cups) 00 pasta flour (12% protein), plus extra for dusting
40g (1½oz/⅓ cup) potato flour (starch)
½ tsp fine sea salt
3 tbsp hot water
1 tbsp vegetable oil

For the clam broth
900ml (32fl oz/3¾ cups) stock of your choice (pages 219–221)
1 tbsp soup or light soy sauce
1 garlic clove, minced
¼ onion, thinly sliced
100g (3½oz) courgettes (zucchini), halved lengthways, then sliced into half-moon shapes
150g (5½oz) potato, sliced in a similar size to the courgette
500g (1lb 2oz) clams, cleaned and purged if necessary

To finish
1 spring onion (scallion), sliced diagonally

To serve
Spicy Chilli Seasoning Sauce (page 225) (optional)

To make the dough, place both flours in a large mixing bowl. Whisk the salt into the hot water to dissolve. Make a well in the middle of the flour and carefully pour in the hot salted water and oil. Using chopsticks or the long handle of a wooden spoon, stir to combine the dry and wet ingredients until you have what resembles rough crumbs. Gently knead the dough for 5 minutes or so, bringing the ingredients together to form a craggy dough, adding a touch more water if you feel it is necessary. Don't worry if the dough still appears rough in places, as we will knead it once more after a short rest. Place the dough in a reusable plastic bag or wrap with clingfilm (plastic wrap). Rest for 10 minutes at room temperature.

Return to the dough. Place it on a stable surface and start kneading again, energetically pressing and stretching with the heels of your hands. Continue until the dough feels supple and the surface appears smooth. It may take 10–15 minutes. Cover the dough again,

then refrigerate for at least 1 hour or preferably overnight. Remove the dough from the fridge 30 minutes before you want to use it to allow it to come back to room temperature.

To prepare the hand-torn noodles, divide the dough in half, so you have a more manageable volume to work with. Keep the second half covered so it doesn't dry out. Lightly flour your surface and start rolling out the first piece into a sheet about 5mm (¼in) thick, lightly dusting with flour as you work. Repeat with the other piece. Cut both sheets into 4cm (1½in) wide strips, then roughly tear each strip into bite-sized pieces. Cover the strips with a tea towel for the time being.

Put your chosen stock in a large, heavy-based saucepan and bring to the boil. Reduce the heat and add the soy sauce, garlic, onion, courgette and potatoes. Let it simmer gently for 10–15 minutes until the vegetables are tender.

WARM NOODLES

Increase the heat to high. Add the clams to the broth, followed by the hand-torn dough, stirring once or twice as you go along. Then simmer for a few minutes until the noodles and clams are cooked through – you will notice the noodles rising up to the surface as they cook. Discard any clams that remain closed.

To serve, divide the noodles between two bowls, ensuring each bowl has a generous amount clams and vegetables. Scatter the spring onion on top.

Serve immediately with spicy chilli seasoning sauce on the side, if you like.

Noodles

Sweet Treats

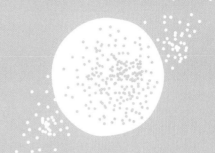

eight

that bittersweet sugar in my throat

The frequency with which my mother cooked lessened as my parents' business grew. Subsequently my memories – the taste of my childhood – no longer lay in the houses we lived in, but rather in the places we ate out. It became more convenient to order pizzas in a couple of nights a week, or have dinners out at nearby local restaurants.

We lived in a two-and-a-half bedroomed apartment in the supposedly up-and-coming area of Seoul that skimmed the stretch of the Han river. My parents were the proud owners of a high-rise apartment. No one really thought that the area was being gentrified, but my mother apparently had a feeling. And she was right. The area, once full of industrial estates and factories, became the hub that connected many places.

Tall, brand-new apartments changed the skylines, and concrete yards were replaced with playgrounds surrounded by trees and benches. We looked out of our balcony to see the stars, but saw the cranes rise high up to the sky at night with twinkling lights, to build high-rise apartments and department stores.

We had a modern kitchen kitted out properly with a gas hob and a tall fridge-freezer.

I had my own bedroom with a Western-style bed and a brand-new computer. The room was neatly arranged with a desk stretching the entire length of the wall and a window that faced the fancy communal elevator. I spent hours on my old, slightly out of tune piano, and dreamt about getting into music school in America one day where our long-distance

cousins supposedly lived. At last, I was allowed to have a couple of hamsters as pets. They ran on the small exercise wheel for ever and ever, day and night; the same way my parents worked their days into often late nights. With their beady red eyes glowing amber in the dark, it used to frighten the life out me. So I stayed away from my bedroom until my mother came home to move them elsewhere.

Everyone in the family became pretty self-sufficient at looking after themselves while the business blossomed and promised us a bigger and better life. I was now responsible for my two siblings while our parents were at work, in the same but different way my father once was as an eldest child. There was a grown-up feeling about it, but I also wanted to find some real fun and freedom hanging out with friends.

I saw my father often tired and stressed, and my mother no longer had time to peel the skin off apples like a nesting snake. Instead, our freezer was filled with ice creams and the fridge was never empty, to make up for their inevitable absence. I knew everything they did was all for us and wasn't resentful, though I wished it was a little different from time to time.

Whilst my father did not consider it a meal if it did not involve a hot steaming bowl of rice or noodles, both my parents liberally welcomed with open arms the rapid arrival of smart bakery chains and restaurants in Seoul back in the '90s. The neon-blue signed 'Paris Baguette' bakery sold dreams filled with picture-perfect cakes layered with fresh cream and cut strawberries. My parents took us to Costco at weekends to browse the new world, where shelves were filled with imported goodies from faraway places we'd never been before. We once or twice went to TGI Fridays for dinner to try out all the weird and wonderful things we'd only seen on television. None of us had a clue what to order or how to eat such things. But my father happily embarrassed himself by asking the young and cool hipster staff to show us how, so that his children would grow up to fit comfortably in a better-cultured society than the small world he grew up in.

My father was the proud owner of an American branded toasted sandwich maker from Costco. We made perfectly triangular-shaped peanut butter and jelly sandwiches with a loaf of sweet milk bread. Sundays were for IMAX movies at the 63 Building. We ate a bucket of Kentucky Fried Chicken with French fries in a newly opened food hall, while he sneaked out by himself to a swanky Japanese udon place just across the hall, because fried chicken wasn't his thing. But he liked the buttery KFC biscuits that came with sweet strawberry jam, so we took a bag home. The waxy crumbs often stuck to the roof of my mouth, but I didn't care; I licked the jam clean out of its cute miniature plastic tub with my tongue, wanting to hold on to the saccharine-sweet sugar high.

Those were the times when I swapped rice for cream-filled fresh buns and snacked on smooth peanut cream-filled sandwiches from the school canteen. I ate them five days in a row if I liked, to savour the sweet bread that tasted like freedom from afar. Everything tasted more intensely seasoned, bursting with excitement that made me feel all the possibilities on the horizon.

The labours of life as an aspiring young family started to present its own problems. Small successes brought bigger opportunities that consumed more of our family time. My father was unaware that I was already a teenager with rising hormones. I did not dream of law schools like my father wanted me to. I wanted to write poems and paint beautiful pictures to tell the stories about my lust for life.

The wedge between my father and me grew deeper and deeper, unable to come to terms with our differences. I did not eat at the same table as him for six months as an act of protest, struggling to forgive the man who seemed so cruel and forceful of his own ideas of what a good daughter should be, or what I ought to become. But it was also my father who instilled the idea that we should absolutely have the best plate of food we could afford. He taught me there was a real pleasure to be found in eating and sharing delicious things together as one. Strange how I can love him so much for that, but yet struggle with the memories of just how hurtful it all was at times.

I know he felt a sense of betrayal from my yearning for creativity. I was wilful and stubborn, and he struggled with the idea that he couldn't 'control' his daughter.

When my daughter was born, I thought carefully about the meaning of responsibility. I swam only to sink deep into the bottom of the ocean, swallowed up by the sheer weight of the words that pressed against my breastbone, heavy and serious. Philip Larkin's poem 'This Be the Verse' was stuck in my head like a broken record. I didn't want to fuck it up or hurt Kiki's feelings. I wanted her to know that I would unconditionally trust her to be her inherent self, and that I would try my damned hardest not to influence her with the glories or the scars of my own upbringing.

I later realized that my mother was barely 21 and my father only just over the other side of 25 when I was born. It became easier to process then, just how overwhelmed they must have felt at times with all the responsibilities of parenthood and their personal ambitions to succeed to honour a good life for us all.

When I was pregnant with my daughter, I went home to Korea to walk the streets I used to call my neighbourhood. It had been four or five years since the last visit as a carefree young and wild thing. Now I had become a woman carrying a child between the bones and flesh of my own body, sharing the blood that is thicker than water. I wanted my unborn child to smell the humid air that always wraps my skin, warm and familiar, and taste the sweet cinnamon-flavoured sugar I used to like licking off chewy doughnuts. I promised her I'd always peel the fruit skins like my mother once did; as thinly and closely as possible to the flesh to savour every bit of goodness together. On the last night before we flew back, I sat by the misty water and stroked my ever-growing bump. I was both petrified and excited. But I particularly wanted to hold on to the memories of small rituals that made my childhood taste bitter-sweet and hoped my then unborn child would feel it bone deep – that this is all of me, and that her tiny particles of bone and flesh belong here.

Sweet Treats

Sweet Rice Doughnuts

This is a popular old-school Korean snack which I think deserves more recognition – strangely, it is very little known outside of Korea. This could be partly to do with the fact that, more often than not, most recipes call for what we call 'wet' rice flour: freshly milled rice flour made from pre-soaked rice.

In traditional baking, wet rice flour was preferred because of its excellence in retaining moisture, resulting in more moist and chewier rice cakes that keep well. However, nowadays, more recipes are being developed using dry flour for the convenience of home baking.

Makes about 20 golf-ball-sized balls

250g (9oz/1⅓ cups) glutinous rice flour
50g (1¾oz/heaped ⅓cup) plain (all-purpose) flour
½ tsp baking powder
½ tsp bicarbonate of soda (baking soda)
40g (1½oz/scant ¼ cup) golden caster (superfine) sugar
½ tsp fine sea salt
30g (1oz) unsalted butter, melted
80ml (3fl oz/⅓cup) warm full-fat milk
150ml (5fl oz/⅔cup) hot water, about 80°C (176°F)
vegetable oil, for deep frying

For the cinnamon sugar
2 tbsp golden caster (superfine) sugar
½ tsp ground cinnamon

Sift both flours, the baking powder and bicarbonate of soda into a large mixing bowl. Add the sugar and salt.

In a pourable and heatproof jug, combine the melted butter and warm milk. Stir this into the flour mix, using a wooden spoon or chopsticks. Gradually pour in the hot water and continue to mix until it resembles rough crumbs. Do this in a few stages as your flour may not need as much water, or might need a touch more, than stated here.

When the dough is cool enough to handle, start bringing the ingredients together by gently kneading until the dough feels supple and the surface is smooth.

Place the dough in a reusable plastic bag or wrap with clingfilm (plastic wrap). Rest in the fridge for at least 1 hour or overnight.

After the dough has rested, divide it into four equal-sized portions so you have a more manageable volume to work with. Work one piece at a time, keeping the remaining dough covered. Shape the dough roughly into a log, then divide it into 5 small golf-ball-sized dough balls. The texture of the dough may feel unusual and a little crumbly. Don't worry if this happens – just squeeze the dough firmly to shape.

Combine the sugar and cinnamon together in a bowl or a rimmed roasting pan. Have another plate or dish ready lined with some kitchen paper.

Fill a saucepan suitable for deep-frying with vegetable oil. It should be filled deep enough to submerge the dough balls but no more than three-quarters full. Heat to 160°C (320°F). If you don't have a thermometer, a cube of bread should brown in 12 seconds. When it reaches 160°C (320°F), turn off the heat and carefully lower a few of the dough balls into the pan, making sure you don't overcrowd the pan. Keep the heat off for 2 minutes. After 2 minutes, the dough will start to move and float a little.

Turn the heat back on and maintain the temperate at 160°C (320°F). Fry the dough balls for 5 minutes, making sure to gently push them down with a heatproof sieve or wire skimmer as they will continuously float up. After 5 minutes, the doughnuts should appear golden brown and cooked through. Transfer to the plate lined with kitchen paper to absorb the excess oil. Continue with the remaining dough balls.

When all the batches are cooked, roll them in the cinnamon sugar while hot and serve immediately.

Sweet Treats

Milk Granita with Sweet Red Beans

Patbingsu

In the height of summer in Seoul, when the scorching city sun beats down hard on skin to turn it red raw, causing flushed cheeks and sticky foreheads, there is only one thing in my mind that will instantly cool me down: a bowl of flaky, shaved ice piled high like a mountain – snow under a sweet mess of soft red beans studded with chewy rice cakes. It hits the throat like a cold shower. Soon your skin wakes up with sharply rising goosebumps and, before you know it, clashing elbows fight to dig spoons into the last puddle of brown-splodged mush. People often say *patbingsu* is best when it is shared, but I could quite happily eat a bucketful alone (standing in the kitchen).

The granita here is built upon the flavours of a shaved ice dessert, which is often layered with sweet condensed milk that trickles through the ice. I never tend to make complicated desserts because I have an incredibly lazy palate when it comes to puddings, so this recipe is as simple as combining all the liquids together and fluffing it up as frequently as it starts to set. I am not ashamed to reach out for tinned aduki beans from the back of the cupboard, which instantly turns my craving into reality with a simple stir of sugar and a slow simmer.

I like to top this liberally with beautiful maraschino liqueur-soaked cherries, including the syrup, to bring it all together with a grown-up edge. Otherwise, use a good old tin of fruit cocktail soaked in syrup.

Combine all the ingredients for the granita in a freezer-safe container, cover and freeze for about 1 hour, or until the ice crystals start to partially set. Scrape round the edges with a fork to shave the surface and make flakes of ice. Repeat the process every half an hour or so for a couple of hours until all the lumps are broken into a slushy-like consistency.

Meanwhile, place the red beans, sugar and water in a small saucepan and bring it to a simmer over a low heat. Give it a good stir and continue to simmer gently for 35 minutes, stirring occasionally. After 35 minutes, the beans will have broken down and be soft but still just about holding their shape. Check for seasoning and adjust it with a touch of honey and salt. The beans should taste sweet but not sickly. Once cooled, transfer to an airtight container and refrigerate.

To serve, divide the flaked milk granita into bowls and spoon over the sweetened red bean paste. Top with one or two maraschino cherries and douse the syrup generously over the granita – leftover cherries can be used for cocktails. Serve immediately and mix everything together before eating.

Serves 4–6

For the granita
400ml (13fl oz/generous 1½ cups) full-fat milk
300ml (10fl oz/1¼ cups) coconut water
200g (7oz) condensed milk
½ tsp sea salt flakes

For the red beans
2 × 400g (14oz) tins of aduki beans, drained and rinsed
4 tbsp golden caster (superfine) sugar
200ml (7fl oz/scant 1 cup) water
clear honey, to taste
sea salt flakes, to taste

To finish
400g (14oz) jar of maraschino cherries (I like the Luxardo brand)

Peanut Butter Cream Bun

This is somewhat reminiscent of the two flavours I used to love as a child: peanut butter cream sandwiches from my old-school canteen and cream buns from the Paris Baguette bakery. The dough here is tenderly crumbed like a soft bun you can squish. They are good for both sweet and savoury fillings, especially for breakfast – in Korea, sweetened milk buns are often named morning *ppang*.

I am not much of a baker and certainly don't have a great deal of skill to make fancy things; what I can guarantee is that the dough is easy enough to cobble together (even more so if you are using a stand mixer) and is tasty. I particularly like the touch of savouriness peanut butter adds to the cream, balanced with sugar and flaked salt. I also think it is a pretty lush treat for the 4pm slump.

Makes 6 buns

150ml (5fl oz/scant ⅔ cup) full-fat milk
40g (1½oz/scant ¼ cup) golden caster (superfine) sugar
½ tsp fine sea salt
250g (9oz/2 cups) strong bread flour
50g (1¾oz/heaped ⅓ cup) plain (all-purpose) flour, plus extra for dusting
1 tsp fast active yeast (quick yeast)
1 egg, lightly whisked
40g (1½oz) unsalted butter, cubed and at room temperature

For the egg wash
1 egg yolk
1 tbsp full-fat milk
a pinch of fine sea salt

For the peanut butter cream
300ml (10fl oz/1¼ cups) fresh double (heavy) cream
100g (3½oz/½ cup) unsalted peanut butter (crunchy or smooth)
4 tbsp icing sugar (confectioners' sugar), plus extra for serving
sea salt flakes, to taste

Pour the milk into a small saucepan and gently warm it up until it reaches about 60°C (140°F). Remove from the heat and whisk in the sugar and salt to dissolve.

Meanwhile, combine both the flours and the dry yeast in a mixing bowl. Slowly pour in the warm milk and sugar mixture. Stir to combine using a wooden spoon or chopsticks. Stir in the egg. Start bringing them together by gently kneading to form a rough dough – it should take about 5 minutes. The dough will feel quite wet to start with but it will come together. I find the 'slap and fold' technique works particularly well to form the dough, so if you're not familiar with the methods, do search online – there are plenty of video tutorials available.

Gradually, add the soft cubed butter to the dough and knead energetically to combine until the butter is evenly incorporated into the dough – about 10–15 minutes. The dough may feel slightly tacky to touch and that is perfectly fine. Shape the dough into a large ball and transfer into a lightly greased bowl. Cover with clingfilm (plastic wrap) and rest it in a warm place for 1–1½ hours until it doubles in volume.

Line a baking tray with parchment paper.

Once the dough has risen, gently push in the middle to knock the air out. Transfer the dough onto a sturdy surface, lightly dusted with flour. Divide the dough into six roughly equal pieces – each should weigh around 90g (3¼oz). Cover the remaining dough and start working on one piece to form a round ball. I like to do this by gently folding the edges of the dough into the centre onto itself, then turning it over to shape it into a tight ball with a smooth and supple surface. Repeat with the rest. Place the dough balls on the lined baking tray, making sure they are evenly spaced out. Cover with clingfilm and rest in a warm place for a further 1 hour until the dough has risen again to almost double in volume.

Combine the ingredients for the egg wash in a bowl.

Preheat a fan oven to 160°C (320°F/gas 4).

→

Sweet Treats

When the dough is ready, lightly and very gently brush the surface with the egg wash twice, allowing a few minutes between washes to give it time to dry. Bake for 18 minutes in the middle of the oven until beautifully shiny and golden. Carefully transfer to a cooling rack.

Meanwhile, place the cream, peanut butter and sugar into a mixing bowl. Whisk together to form a spreadable cream consistency – about 3 minutes. Fold in a pinch of flaky salt to taste: for me, this is about $\frac{1}{4}$ teaspoon.

Once the buns have cooled completely, using a sharp bread knife, make a cut across the middle from the top about two-thirds of the way down, but not all the way through. Hold the roll in your less dominant hand to allow the middle to open. Scoop in about two tablespoons of peanut butter cream to fill. Smooth out the edges, if you like, with the flat edge of a small knife (a palette or butter knife are good for this). Lightly dust with icing sugar and serve immediately.

Honey Panna Cotta with Instant Coffee Caramel

I used to make iced coffees with instant coffee granules for my mother every summer. She returned home from work in the early hours of the evening, when the hot and humid August sun sits low and tapers softly into charming golden light. Her pale-pink-toned face looked hot with rosy-red cheeks. I had seen many times before how she liked to gulp down her thirst with slushy toffee-brown-coloured coffee; I would stir up a mixing bowl full of murky liquid without knowing what it really tasted like, but assuming by the shade of brown that it was 'right'. My mother drank it straight from the bowl, standing in the kitchen where the fading sun lit her face with a warm glow, leaving me with her big smile and rare praise to savour. I know it made me feel good, but I never quite knew what it might mean for her and how it made her feel at the time, until I had my own child hand me one of her snacks once, saying, 'For you, Mummy.'

And I grew up to love the taste of coffee, enough to get through the whole tub of Häagen-Dazs coffee-flavoured ice-cream from the 24-hour convenience stores, straight out of the tub throughout my adolescence. I drank plenty of iced coffees in summer, often thinking about how my mother took hers: bitterly strong with lots of sugar and whitened with powdered coffee creamer, which smelled both sweet and burnt – in a nice way.

Set cream here is flavoured subtly with instant coffee, inspired by my memories, with coffee caramel sauce to emulate the sense of sweet and burnt. You will have some caramel sauce left over; it will keep well for a couple of weeks and is good poured over vanilla ice-cream.

Neutrally flavoured honey pairs better, which allows the cream to coherently carry the coffee notes. It is an easy dessert to make – one that I can reliably return to. Not too sweet, not too bitter: just enough of everything to remind me of my mother, and every lasting bit of summer back home.

You will need 4 × 150ml (5fl oz/⅔ cup) moulds, cups or equivalent.

To make the coffee caramel, place half the cream and the tablespoon of instant coffee in a small saucepan to warm up, whisking constantly to dissolve the coffee. As soon as it has dissolved, remove from the heat and combine with the rest of the cream. Set aside.

Place the sugar and water in a heavy-based saucepan, along with the lime zest and lime juice. Swirl the pan around a little so the sugar is saturated in liquid. Bring to a simmer over a medium heat without disturbing the pan too much. After about 7 minutes or so, the sugar should have turned golden brown in colour. Check the true colour of caramelized sugar by taking a small amount onto a white plate, as it always looks darker in the pan. Remove from the heat and carefully whisk in the double cream and coffee mixture. It may spit a little initially, so keep the pan at a distance. Continue whisking until well combined, then add a good pinch of salt to taste – not so much to make salted caramel, but more to balance the flavour to accentuate the sweetness. When done, set aside.

→

Serves 4

For the coffee caramel
5 tbsp double (heavy) cream
1 tbsp instant coffee
100g (3½oz/½ cup) golden caster (superfine) sugar
3 tbsp water
1 unwaxed lime, zest and juice
a pinch of sea salt flakes

For the panna cotta
2 × 2g leaves of gelatine
225ml (8fl oz/1 cup) double (heavy) cream
225ml (8fl oz/1 cup) full-fat milk
55g (2oz) raw honey
1 tbsp instant coffee
vegetable oil, for greasing
crushed chocolate-covered coffee beans, for garnish (optional)

To make the panna cotta, soak the gelatine leaves in cold water to soften. Place the cream, full-fat milk, honey and instant coffee in a small saucepan over a low heat. Heat gently to bring to barely simmering, stirring occasionally for about 5 minutes until the mixture feels warm and the honey is fully incorporated. Remove from the heat and leave it to cool down slightly: it should feel warm to the touch, but not too hot or cold, in order for the gelatine leaves to set properly.

Remove the gelatine leaves from the water and squeeze to remove excess moisture. Stir the gelatine leaves into the warm cream and milk mixture to dissolve. Once combined, pass it through a fine sieve into a clean jug.

Lightly grease the inside of four small coffee cups, ramekins or moulds of your choice; this will help to invert the set cream onto the plate more easily. (If you don't plan to turn them out when serving then there is no need to grease.)

Place 1 heaped spoonful, about 15g (½oz), of caramel mixture into each mould. Gently tap the bottom of the mould against the worktop to even out – any leftover caramel can be refrigerated in an airtight container for a couple of weeks. Divide the cream mixture between the four moulds, cool and cover, then refrigerate to set for at least 4 hours or overnight.

To serve, dip the base of the dishes briefly in boiling water to warm and loosen the set cream, then carefully invert onto plates. You may need to give them a little shake to encourage them to slide out graciously. Serve with a touch more coffee caramel sauce, if you like, and crushed chocolate-covered coffee beans, if using.

Ginger Tea

When the mornings start to rise with chillier air that feels fresher on the lungs and cooler on the skin, I know we're on the cusp of winter in London. The air feels damp and there is the smell of smoke from the houses with working chimneys burning wood. Early hours are still dark enough to light candles that trail the faint whiff of burnt matchsticks. It's the time at which I begin to put rice porridges on for slow breakfast at the weekend, and snuggle up a little closer to my child in bed to feel cosy. And soon, the kitchen warms up, glowing under the candle lights that make everything look softer and prettier.

It is this tea I crave in the mornings at this time of year. Not the milk-stirred kind but invigoratingly spicy ginger tea that makes me feel the tickling heat from the inside. It can even be served with a slice of lemon to perfume. My mother loved her tea. She dried clementine skins on top of the oil heater (or on the heated floors at home) and kept her pot of hot water to drink endless cups of tea to warm up in winter. Everywhere she went smelled like a garden full of citrus fruits, with the occasional scent of cinnamon-spiced ginger tea.

Ginger syrup does take some time to make but isn't too difficult. It keeps well in the fridge – if you can refrain from drinking it all up too quickly. Ginger is best peeled with a teaspoon to gently scrape off the skin as thinly as possible. You will need a muslin or cheesecloth to separate the pulp and liquid. The pulp can be preserved, completely saturated with sake, to be used for cooking – use a sterilized jar and store in the fridge. Or dehydrate in a very low oven, then grind to a fine powder to make ground ginger.

Makes enough to fill a 500ml (17fl oz/ 2 cups) sterilized and heatproof jar

500g (1lb 2oz) ginger root
½ Asian pear, peeled, cored and cut into chunks
100ml (3½fl oz/scant ½ cup) water
300g (10½oz/1½ cups) golden granulated sugar
75g (2½oz) raw honey
1 cinnamon stick, about 5cm (2in) long

To peel the ginger, gently scrape off the skin with a teaspoon. Rinse with cold water and slice roughly. Place the ginger, pear and water in a high-speed blender or food processor, and blend until smooth.

Set a fine sieve over a bowl and lay the muslin or cheesecloth over the sieve. Carefully pour the puréed ginger into the cloth. Wrap tightly and squeeze to wring out as much liquid as possible, pressing on the solids. Once all the juice from the puréed ginger is collected, discard the pulp (or preserve as mentioned above) and leave the bowl of juice to sit for 1 hour completely undisturbed. You want to separate the starch from the liquid, which will pool at the bottom of the bowl.

After 1 hour, carefully pour the clear juice into a heavy-based saucepan, making sure not to pour in the starch gathered at the bottom. As soon as you see the pale yellowy white starch, stop. Discard the starch. Add the sugar, honey and cinnamon stick to the pan. Bring to a simmer over a medium heat, then lower the heat and simmer for 1 hour, stirring occasionally. As the syrup reduces and thickens, you will notice small bubbles bloom. When it reaches syrupy consistency to coat the back of the spoon, it is done – the density of syrup will feel quite loose but will thicken further as it cools.

Discard the cinnamon stick and leave the syrup to cool slightly. Transfer to a sterilized jar and store in the fridge. It should keep for up to one year.

To serve, stir a couple of teaspoonfuls of syrup into a mugful of hot water, with or without a squeeze of lemon.

Stocks + Condiments

nine

useful stocks and condiments
to brighten up the rice table

In this chapter I have collected together a few basic recipes that form the backbone of many of the recipes in the book, or provide traditional dishes to enliven your rice table.

Yuksu

Homemade stock – or *yuksu* – is an essential part of Korean home cooking that forms the basis of many dishes. Many home cooks instinctively know how to make a few simple stocks. And for those with time in short supply, conveniently weighed out pouches of *yuksu* ingredients can be purchased as easily as buying tea bags, so you can simply steep them in water at home.

Less familiar ingredients in Korean stocks and methods might make it look like a daunting task. But once you can break down the basics, making stock at home really is not too difficult at all. I think it's the case of building the muscle memory so we can form a habit of doing it again and again until the process feels less foreign.

The stocks I share here can be used for most of the recipes interchangeably across the book, unless the recipe specifies otherwise. Korean stocks generally taste mild, so they can work harmoniously with the flavours and more complex seasoning of fermented products. Where recipes use meat as a main ingredient to flavour soups and stews, I mostly use water to allow the true taste of the meat to come through. But the use of stock can also play an interesting role in giving the dish a backbone to develop layers of unique flavours and textures that yield complex depth and a more lived-in finish to a dish. Stock can also add volume to a dish, making it feel more silky and weightier (in a good way) than water in the mouth.

Quick Stock

The easiest and simplest way to make a stock is to store this concoction of liquid overnight in the fridge to slowly extract the flavour. I keep a litre (2-pint) jar in the fridge so the cold-brewed stock can be used as a quick stock straight from the fridge. This is the most basic recipe I use, which can be multiplied or halved easily depending on your needs.

Combine all the ingredients in a jug or bottle. Let it sit in the fridge overnight.

If you have time, you could pour the contents of the jug into a saucepan to simmer gently for 15 minutes to maximize the flavour.

Strain through a fine sieve before using. Discard the dasima and reserve the rehydrated mushrooms for later use – they can be thrown into soups and stir-fries.

Makes 1 litre (34fl oz/ 4 cups)

two 5 × 7.5cm (2 × 3in) sheets of *dasima* (dried kelp)
10g (⅓oz) dried shiitake mushrooms
1 litre (34fl oz/4 cups) water

Dasima + Mushroom Stock

Consider this as an upgrade from the cold-brewed quick stock on the previous page. The key is to simmer very gently to allow the flavours to slowly amalgamate into one another, to give the stock more depth and a rounded finish. The addition of alliums lends subtle background sweetness, and the earthiness of the mushrooms blooms as they steep in the warm bath. I adore its subtlety.

Makes about 2.6 litres (88fl oz/10¾ cups)

30g (1oz) dried shiitake mushrooms
six 5 × 7.5cm (2 × 3in) sheets of *dasima* (dried kelp)
3 litres (100fl oz/12 cups) water
100g (3½oz) leek
1 onion, halved with skin left on
1 tbsp black peppercorns

If time allows, place the dried shiitake mushrooms and *dasima* in a lidded stockpot along with the water the night before, so they can slowly rehydrate. The pot can be kept at room temperature: leave somewhere cool in the kitchen.

If you soaked the mushrooms and *dasima* overnight, add the rest of the ingredients to the stockpot. Otherwise, begin the process by adding all the ingredients into a stockpot. Place the stockpot over a medium heat with the lid on ajar and bring to a very gentle simmer (never boil). Then reduce the heat as low as possible and keep it barely simmering for 1 hour – the liquid in the pot should look almost still.

You may want to skim off any scum that gathers around the pan, but don't fret too much. A low and slow simmer will help to prevent scum emulsifying into the stock.

After 1 hour, remove from the heat. Leave it to rest to cool completely. Lift out the mushrooms and reserve – they can be tossed into soups and stews. Remove the chunks of vegetable and discard. Carefully strain the stock through a fine sieve into a jug or a container and discard any solids. Store in the fridge. It should keep well for three days without compromising on quality too much. Or freeze the stock to keep for a month.

Anchovy Stock

This is not a fishy stock; it is a stock subtly flavoured with ocean-like saltiness. Traditionally, the gut (the black sac that sits on the underside of the belly) and sometimes also the head were discarded before the rest was thrown into the stock. However, there is an argument as to whether the removal of dried anchovy guts is necessary. Some people seem to think that when whole anchovies are steeped slowly over a low heat, the subtle bitterness can actually work to add flavour – I think it depends on preference.

Dry roasting of the anchovies is an important step to prevent the stock from imparting an unpleasant fishy taste, so don't skip it. Korean dried anchovies can be found in the freezer section in Asian grocers. They can be used from frozen.

Try maintaining the pot at about 90°C (194°F) – the surface of the pot will look almost still and you will see tiny bubbles rising intermittently.

If time allows, place the *dasima* in a lidded stockpot with the water the night before, so it can steep to slowly rehydrate. It can be kept at room temperature: leave somewhere cool in the kitchen.

To prepare the anchovies, pull off the head and remove the guts by gently separating the body apart. Discard the guts. Place the head and body parts of the anchovies in a saucepan. Dry roast for about 2 minutes over a medium heat until you can smell the aroma of fish. You may hear a soft crackly sound from the pan. Remove from the heat to cool slightly.

If you soaked the *dasima* overnight, add the anchovies to the stockpot along with the rest of the ingredients. Otherwise, transfer the dry roasted anchovies to a stockpot and add the *dasima* and water, along with the rest of the ingredients.

Place the stockpot over a medium heat with the lid on ajar and bring to a very gentle simmer (never boil). Then reduce the heat as low as possible and keep it barely simmering for 1 hour – the liquid in the pot should look almost still. You may want to skim off any scum that gathers around the pan occasionally. Don't fret too much though, as a low and slow simmer will help to prevent scum emulsifying into the stock – you will get a clear stock.

After 1 hour, remove from the heat. Leave it to rest to cool completely. Lift out the chunks of vegetable and discard. Carefully strain the stock through a fine sieve into a jug or a container and discard the solids. Then store in the fridge. It should keep well for three days without compromising on quality too much. Or freeze the stock to keep for a month.

Makes about 2.6 litres (88fl oz /10¾ cups)

three 5 × 7.5cm (2 × 3in) sheets of *dasima* (dried kelp)
3 litres (100fl oz/12 cups) water
60g (2oz) large dried anchovies
100g (3½oz) leek
100g (3½oz) daikon radish, left as a chunk
1 onion, halved with the skin left on
1 tbsp black peppercorns
2 tbsp sake

Ssam Sauce

Ssamjang

Makes about 135g (4½oz)

2 tbsp *doenjang* (Korean fermented bean paste)
1 tbsp *gochujang* (Korean red chilli paste)
1 tbsp rice vinegar
1 tbsp toasted sesame oil
1 tsp golden granulated sugar
1 tsp *gochugaru* (Korean red pepper flakes)
2 tsp blackstrap molasses
1 tsp toasted white sesame seeds
2 garlic cloves, minced
1 spring onion (scallion), minced

I can't imagine a spread of *ssam* (page 124) without a decent *ssamjang*. This sauce lends a deeply assertive saltiness laced with smoky heat; it's incredibly robust and versatile.

Blackstrap molasses (found in most health food stores) used here isn't a typical Korean ingredient, but I adore its bitter sweetness which pairs brilliantly with earthy *doenjang*, complementing the sauce with a more balanced finish.

Whist the sauce can be consumed more or less immediately, it will benefit from being made in advance – at least a day ahead. When it's left to mature in the fridge, the sharp edges of raw ingredients start to soften; its colour deepens and the overall flavour greatly improves. Stored in an airtight container, it will keep well for two weeks in the fridge.

-

Combine all the ingredients in an airtight container and refrigerate.

Chive Dipping Sauce

Cho Ganjang

Serves 1–2

1 tbsp soy sauce
1 tbsp rice vinegar
1 tbsp water
1 tsp golden granulated sugar
1 tsp snipped chives
½ tsp *gochugaru* (Korean red pepper flakes) optional

I think fried food needs a piquant sauce to cut through the richness. Well-balanced salty acidity here adds pleasing tartness and an extra layer of seasoning to any fried dishes, from grease-licked savoury pancakes to deep-fried fritters. The recipe here is a starting point that you can tweak to build more characters; add fiery chopped chilli for heat, or chopped onions to enjoy the refreshing taste of allium and so on.

-

Combine all the ingredients in a small mixing bowl, before serving.

Stocks + Condiments

Stir-Fried Gochujang Sauce

Yakgochujang

Makes about 530g (1lb 3oz)

1 tbsp vegetable oil
½ onion, minced
a pinch of sea salt flakes
2 tbsp golden granulated sugar
1 tbsp sake
2 tbsp *gochugaru* (Korean red pepper flakes)
200g (7oz) *gochujang* (Korean red chilli paste)
2 tbsp neutral-tasting raw honey
2 tbsp toasted sesame oil
1 tbsp toasted white sesame seeds, lightly ground

For the beef
200g (7oz) minced (ground) beef
¼ Asian pear, peeled, cored and puréed
½ tsp grated ginger root
2 garlic cloves, minced
2 spring onions (scallions), minced
1 tsp golden granulated sugar
1 tsp mirin
2 tsp soy sauce
1 tsp toasted sesame seeds
¼ tsp freshly cracked black pepper

This stir-fried *gochujang* sauce studded with beef is enjoyed in small quantities on the side of rice to lift one's wilting palate. Sweetened with sugar and honey, the thick paste-like sauce is packed full of mouthwatering heat that is quite simply addictive. Use to season *Bibimbap* (page 166), to accompany *ssam* or just serve a good dollop on top of plain steamed rice. The sauce keeps incredibly well. Stored in an airtight container, it'll keep well for three weeks in the fridge.

Combine all the ingredients for the beef in a mixing bowl.

Heat the vegetable oil in a sauté pan over a low heat. Add the onion, along with the pinch of salt and sauté gently for 5 minutes to soften. Increase the heat to medium and stir in the beef. Stir frequently and cook for a further 5 minutes or so until the pan appears dry – browning is not important here, just cook it down until there is no sign of moisture. Add the sugar and sake, and cook for a minute or so to melt the sugar and cook off the sake. Lower the heat and stir in the *gochugaru* and *gochujang*. Fry very gently for 3 minutes, stirring frequently to incorporate. Stir in the honey, sesame oil and ground sesame seeds.

Let it cool completely. Transfer to an airtight container and refrigerate.

Chilli Oil

Gochu Gireum

**Makes enough to fill a 150ml (5fl oz/scant ⅔cup)
sterilized and heatproof jar**

200ml (7fl oz/scant 1 cup) vegetable oil
20g (¾oz) garlic cloves, minced
15g (½oz) ginger root, sliced
60g (2oz) leek, thinly sliced
50g (1¾oz) *gochugaru* (Korean red pepper flakes)

This is a versatile chilli oil that can be
used for cooking. It is particularly useful for
Soft Tofu Stew with Clams (page 118), which
gives the dish a foundation heat. Laced with
beautiful leek flavour, it can be used liberally
to add a gentle humming heat. Stored in an
airtight container, it'll keep well for a month
in the fridge.

-

Put the vegetable oil, garlic, ginger and leek
in a cold heavy-based saucepan. Place the pan
over a low heat and steep the alliums in oil to fry
very gently until the leeks turn golden – about
18 minutes. You should notice the tiny bubbles
rising on the surface, which should indicate the
temperature has risen to about 120°C (248°F).

Stir in the *gochugaru* and lower the heat. Cook
for 3 minutes to release the flavour of the chilli,
until the *gochugaru* turns deep mahogany red
but not burnt. Remove from the heat. Cool
slightly, then pass through a fine sieve lined
with a muslin or cheesecloth, or a paper coffee
filter, into a heatproof jug. Transfer to a sterilized
jar or bottle. Cool completely and refrigerate.

Spicy Chilli Seasoning Sauce

Dadaegi

Makes about 100g (3½oz)

2 tbsp *gochugaru* (Korean red pepper flakes)
1 tbsp soy sauce
1 tbsp toasted sesame oil
1 tbsp fish sauce
1 tsp golden granulated sugar
1 tsp toasted white sesame seeds
¼ tsp freshly ground white pepper
1 garlic clove, minced
1 spring onion (scallion), finely chopped
1 tbsp chopped mild red chilli (optional)

Dadaegi is an all-purpose seasoning often
used to flavour mild brothy noodle dishes. It has
foreground saltiness which is laced with cooling
allium and varying degrees of heat, depending
on the amount and types of chilli used. Prepare
it in advance as it is best left to sit in the fridge
to mature and develop flavour. Stored in airtight
container, it will keep well for a week.

-

Combine all the ingredients in an airtight
container and refrigerate.

Writing, for the most part, doesn't come all that easily or naturally to me.

But I do enjoy getting lost in the act of articulating my thoughts and dreams into words that feel much more solid, so I can actively let go of those wandering thoughts to put my mind – that forever seems to struggle to sleep – at ease. Once written down, it no longer needs to be tended, but becomes something I can freely come back to when I choose. And perhaps in time, over time, to realize what exactly it was that made me feel such things or made me see that day the way I did.

I find freedom in writing in the same way that cooking allows me to feel grounded and connected to life around me. My words are elaborate and descriptive, and I know it isn't everyone's favourite cup of tea, but this is the way I see the world around me. I sob my eyes out watching the *X-Factor* contestants chasing their dreams, which my husband thinks 'a little weird'. I love the smell of sun cream on my skin, which almost makes me feel

my sand-covered bare feet treading the ocean. And damp smoky wood always reminds me of our happy feral days in the field camping with our then barely six-month-old child.

Mostly, I try to remember the small things because they reveal so much more than just a place, or the things we ate. The smell of people, how the air felt, if there was any breeze, if I was merrily tipsy or if I was missing home. It is all those small things that build our bones and grow our bodies. They live in the blood that runs in our veins and in the air that we breathe. We share our food and experiences with people who cross our paths through our lifetime, so we can learn and grow and morph into rounder human beings.

My now seven-year-old hasn't yet fully explored my home 5,000 miles away, and barely recognizes my parents as grandparents. I am sometimes scared that I may never be able to give enough of what makes her half Korean. In a way, I am

frightened about memories fading and disappearing into the bottom of the ocean to be forgotten.

So here is the book that I've tried to write as well as I could to record the recipes that belong to both my mother's and my very ordinary kitchen. These are the stories that I felt compelled to tell, so my daughter knows that I really, really tried, in the hope that I can put away that fear with words that I know will be here forever for us to look at together. I would like her to know that this is how it all started and to remember the kitchen was where our love blossomed and spoke thousands of words, in the same way she knows mummy cooks the best rice and it is always best to ask daddy for Nutella-slathered toast because daddy gives her a big spoonful on the side with a little wink.

My dearest Kiki, while I raise you, I raise a stronger woman in me.

Index

Index   231

Thank You

I once said to my Polish friend Binia that I had a dream of writing a book but I was unsure if I could, as English is my second language. She gently slammed the table with vigour, and told me that beautiful sentences don't need fancy words, but an honest heart. She was an incredible academic and artist, with a lifetime of fascinating stories that could be shown in movies. She and her partner Bob welcomed me into their home with open arms for late night conversations about art, life and family. It was there, I first tasted smoked Polish sausage stew made with dried fruit, which gave it a beautifully sweet and jammy edge. We drank many bottles of fruity red wine from their wine collection, read beautiful lines from old cookbooks and listened to old vinyls that reminded me of my father. It was Bob who walked me down the aisle when my parents couldn't make it to my wedding. During the moments when I felt uncertain about my ability to write this book, I reminded myself of Binia's words. This book perhaps wouldn't be here if it wasn't for their love and encouragement. Thank you Bob, and rest your soul in peace, Binia – you are very much of an important part of this book.

Emily, thank you for believing in my story and helping me shape the dreams in my head into words I can share with others. I am blessed to be working with you.

Everyone, especially the team behind the scenes at Quadrille, I am indebted to you all, for not only giving me the opportunity to write my dream book, but also for the creative freedom you've given me.

Harriet, I am forever grateful to you for trusting my vision – thank you for seeing something in me.

Claire and Lucy, thank you so much for bringing to life my vision of the quiet beauty of simplicity.

Tamara, I don't know how I got so lucky but having you create your magic was the most perfect thing. Thank you so much for making my food look as gloriously messy and delicious as it is.

Emma, thank you for helping us on the first day. And Charlotte, you are truly a wonder woman. Thank you for every big and small thing you did to make the shoot run so smoothly.

Rachel, thank you for the gorgeous props and being so open and considerate with your approach. The images are as calm and serene as they are because of you.

Wendy, I have learnt so much from the process back and forth with you. Thank you so much for being patient with me and helping my words carry better meaning.

Joyce, Chris and Freddie, thank you for the endless coffees, cocktails, recipe tastings and playdates. Joyce, your encouragement and enthusiasm for my cooking helped me get through some of the most difficult days of writing. I am so lucky to call you a friend. Page 179 is for you, Chris.

Hazel, thank you so much for looking after Kiki; for always being readily available for us whenever we needed help. I don't know how we'd have coped otherwise.

To my family back home, especially my parents, you let me go and see the world and trusted me to be just me. Your love is quiet but infinite. Thank you so much for giving me the gift of experience. I am proud of my upbringing.

Vince, without you, there would not be a book for Kiki. I am forever in awe of the way you carry yourself with such grace and bravery while battling with big C. You are the family we chose and Kiki is so lucky to call you 'uncle Vince'.

Toby, thank you for giving me the luxury of time to write this book and making my visions come alive – the photos are beautiful. And Kiki, you make me want to be a better person every day. Team Scott, we did it the bestest. X

Managing Director Sarah Lavelle
Commissioning Editor Harriet Webster
Copy Editor Wendy Hobson
Art Directior Claire Rochford
Designer Studio Polka
Photographer Toby Scott
Food Stylist Tamara Vos
Prop Stylist Rachel Vere
Head of Production Stephen Lang
Production Controller Gary Hayes

First published in 2023 by Quadrille,
an imprint of Hardie Grant Publishing

Quadrille
52–54 Southwark Street
London SE1 1UN
quadrille.com

ISBN: 978 1 78713 896 4

Printed in China